LOSING OURSELVES

Losing Ourselves

LEARNING TO LIVE
WITHOUT A SELF

JAY L. GARFIELD

PRINCETON UNIVERSITY PRESS

PRINCETON & OXFORD

Published by Princeton University Press
41 William Street, Princeton, New Jersey 08540
99 Banbury Road, Oxford OX2 6JX

press.princeton.edu

All Rights Reserved

Library of Congress Cataloging-in-Publication Data

Names: Garfield, Jay L., 1955– author.
Title: Losing ourselves : learning to live without a self / Jay L. Garfield.
Description: Princeton : Princeton University Press, [2022] |
    Includes bibliographical references and index.
Identifiers: LCCN 2021053549 (print) | LCCN 2021053550 (ebook) |
    ISBN 9780691220284 (hardback : acid-free paper) |
    ISBN 9780691220291 (ebook)
Subjects: LCSH: Self (Philosophy) | Buddhism—Doctrines. | BISAC:
    PHILOSOPHY / Buddhist | SELF-HELP / Personal Growth / General
Classification: LCC BD438.5 .G385 2022 (print) | LCC BD438.5
    (ebook) | DDC 126—dc23/eng/20211207
LC record available at https://lccn.loc.gov/2021053549
LC ebook record available at https://lccn.loc.gov/2021053550

British Library Cataloging-in-Publication Data is available

Editorial: Rob Tempio & Matt Rohal
Production Editorial: Ali Parrington
Jacket Design: Chris Ferrante
Production: Erin Suydam
Publicity: Alyssa Sanford & Carmen Jimenez
Copyeditor: Jodi Beder

Jacket art: M.C. Escher, *Rind* © 2021 The M.C. Escher Company,
the Netherlands. All rights reserved. www.mcescher.com

This book has been composed in Arno

Printed on acid-free paper. ∞

Printed in the United States of America

10 9 8 7 6 5 4 3 2 1

In Memory of Sandy Huntington,
Friend, Colleague, and
Companion in Cross-Cultural Philosophy

CONTENTS

PREFACE

THIS BOOK is a reflection on selflessness, that is, on what it is to be a *person*, but not to be a *self*. My initial focus will be metaphysical: an exploration of what kinds of things we *are*, and of what kinds of things we *are not*. But the real point of this exploration will emerge towards the end of the book, when we turn to the ethical import of the nonexistence of the self, and what it means for our understanding of our place in the world. I will be arguing explicitly for a position that many may think flies in the face of common sense, *viz.*, that we *are not* selves, nor do we *have* selves. I will not argue that we do not *exist*. That would be madness. But I will argue that we exist not as selves, but as persons. I hope that my argument, to the extent that it is convincing, also persuades you that too often what masquerades as common sense is in fact nonsense. It follows from this that any philosophical program that takes our commonsense intuitions for granted, and then takes as its task to defend them by elucidating them, or by making them more precise, may simply ramify confusion instead of generating clarity.

Some may react to this discussion by thinking that I am drawing a purely verbal distinction that reflects no real philosophical difference, and so think that I am devoting too much ink to making a trivial lexical point; that I am merely arguing for the substitution of one of a pair of synonyms for the other. Others might think that in arguing against the view that we are, or have, selves, I am arguing against a straw man, a position that nobody in fact believes. I hope to convince you that neither is the case, that these terms have very different meanings, that many people—whether professional philosophers or not—take themselves to be selves and not persons in the relevant sense, and that they are wrong to do so. That is, the distinction to which I will draw your attention is a real one, and the position against which I am arguing is no straw man.

The ideas that I will develop are inspired by my long engagement with two philosophers, one Indian and one Scottish: Candrakīrti (c. 600–650 CE) and David Hume (1711–1776 CE). Candrakīrti was a Buddhist scholar and a partisan of the Middle Way School of Mahāyāna Buddhist philosophy. He was distinctive in his defense both of the robust reality of the world we inhabit, and of the view that despite—or more accurately, because of—the fact that that it is real, our own existence and that of the objects and institutions that surround us is merely *conventional*, dependent upon the way we think, and the way we talk. He argued that although we might take ourselves to be *selves* that exist independent of and prior to these conventions, this is an illusion; instead, he argued, these practices constitute us as *persons*. All of this might sound a bit incoherent and even mystical, but as we continue our investigation, its plausibility—and, I hope, its correctness—will emerge.

Just over 1,000 years after Candrakīrti's death, David Hume, in Scotland, defended strikingly similar views. He, like Candrakīrti, argued that we must take the reality of the world around us for granted; he also argued that we are systematically confused if we take our own existence, and that of the world around us, to be prior to and independent of our conventions—our ways of acting, talking, and thinking. Hume also argued that although we have a persistent illusion of being *seslves*, we are

LSI AE conclusion
My book is placed in terms
of discipline remarks
Philosophis association

instead constituted as persons in the context of our interactions
with one another and of the practices that enable those interactions. Although many have thought of Hume's position as interesting only as a straw man to attack, I again hope that as we proceed, its plausibility and indeed its correctness will emerge.

The fact that although Candrakīrti was a Buddhist monk and
Hume was a persistent critic of religion in a Christian country,
they developed strikingly similar accounts of personhood as
well as strikingly similar critiques of the idea of the self is probably no accident: it is highly likely that each account originated
in a shared skeptical tradition, with roots both in the classical
Greek Pyrrhonian tradition and in Indian Buddhism, traditions
that were in contact with one another.[1] But my aim is neither
to compare Hume's and Candrakīrti's ideas and arguments, nor
to present a systematic analysis of their views. Nor is this an
exposition of Buddhist positions on the self. I have undertaken
these tasks elsewhere.[2] Instead, my aim is to develop and to
defend the idea of personhood on its own terms in the absence
of any self, and to explore its ramifications. I will do so in dialogue with both classical and contemporary discussions of this
issue. I will draw freely on Indian and Euro-American texts,
arguments, and ideas. I think that this is the right way to do
philosophy: we should find ideas and conversation partners in
every one of the world's intellectual traditions, and we should
resist even the implicit parochialism that is reflected in attention only to our own cultural context. But this is not meant to
be a book on the history of philosophy, and still less a text in
comparative philosophy; it is merely the exploration of an idea
in conversation with a wide a range of partners. I will therefore
not spend much time doing textual work, except where necessary to make that conversation clear. I do hope, though, that
this discussion demonstrates in part the value of entering into

conversation with multiple traditions when we ask philosophical questions.

I take the topic of what we are to be one of the first importance for at least two reasons. First, I think that a central part of the human project—as Socrates and Plato emphasized in classical Greece, and as the authors of the Upaniṣads emphasized in classical India—is to know ourselves. That is, we think philosophically in order to come to know what kinds of things we are, and how we fit into the social and biological world around us. Second, we are hyper-social animals—animals who recognize and respect norms, including moral norms. Indeed, our moral commitments are at the very heart of who we take ourselves to be.[3] We are unable to countenance immorality, and we each feel a demand to conduct our lives in ways we recognize as ethical. We therefore require a self-understanding that makes our moral life comprehensible. I believe that the illusion that we are selves undermines ethical cultivation and moral vision, and that coming to understand ourselves as persons facilitates a more salutary, mature moral engagement with those around us. For this reason alone, it is important to shed the illusion of the self and to come to terms with our identities as persons.

My goal in this short book is to defend what I take to be a correct position, or at least an interesting one. I cannot provide a complete survey of the issues relevant to this question, let alone definitive solutions to any philosophical questions. In particular, there are fascinating and important questions about how to extend these ideas in order to understand the role of such phenomena as race, gender, and sexuality in the construction of our identities; these will have to be addressed on another occasion. Nor will I venture a careful history of thought about the self and the person, either in Asian or in Western traditions. Others have done that well. There is a vast literature to explore

if one is interested in the self and in our identity. I will nod towards some of that literature in the course of this discussion, but I will try to keep the account as uncluttered as possible, so as to make this an easy read. Professional philosophers know where to find more. I include references that will guide those not already immersed in this literature to some of the most important work of my interlocutors. And I hope that this short book stimulates some of my readers to go deeper into this question in conversation with the texts—both classical and contemporary—to which I refer.

ACKNOWLEDGMENTS

MY THOUGHTS regarding the self and the person reflect not only my study of Candrakīrti and Hume, but also years of productive dialogue with many friends and colleagues in philosophy and Buddhist studies. Some of these colleagues share my views, but many, while sharing my preoccupation with these questions, disagree sharply with me. I am grateful to them for forcing me to confront difficulties with my position and to defend it with greater force and clarity. After all, every philosopher needs friends on both sides of any issue. I acknowledge in particular Dan Arnold, Anita Avramides, Don Baxter, Christian Coseru, Angela Coventry, Georges Dreyfus, Douglas Duckworth, Jonardon Ganeri, Sandy Huntington, Constance Kassor, Kathryn Lindeman, Guy Newland, Hsueh Qu, Vasudevi Reddy, Mark Siderits, Nico Silins, Geshe Yeshes Thabkhas, Evan Thompson, Tom Tillemans, and Dan Zahavi.

I want to thank Evan Thompson in particular for years of friendly, but energetic, debate about these questions. I have learned a great deal from Evan, and much of my thinking has crystallized in our interchanges. I also want to acknowledge that my first musings about Hume and Candrakīrti on the self and the person were in the context of Constance Kassor's work on her excellent honors thesis on that topic. I learned a lot from her, and her insights inform this work. Thanks to Eyal Aviv, Blaine Garson, Constance Kassor, Guy Newland, Shaun

Nichols, Graham Priest, Andy Rotman, Robert Sharf, Roy Tzohar, Jan Westerhoff, and two anonymous readers for very helpful comments on earlier drafts.

Thanks to the Five College Buddhist Studies Faculty Seminar—a venue in which many of my ideas germinate—for a spirited discussion of this manuscript that led to important improvements. In particular, I note the valuable suggestions from Peter Gregory, Jamie Hubbard, Sonam Kachru, Constance Kassor, Sara McClintock, Kristin McCulloch, Tim McNeil, Cat Prueitt, Karl Schmid, and Ajay Sinha. And I am very grateful to my dedicated team of research assistants—Kristina Chiu, Molly McPartlin, and Hallie Jane Richeson—for their insightful and sound critical commentary and for their careful editorial work. This book is much better for their contributions.

Finally, I thank Rob Tempio of the Princeton University Press for the idea of writing this book in the first place, and for sage guidance and critique as the project has developed, and Jodi Beder for improving this book in the editorial process.

LOSING OURSELVES

1

Who Do You Think You Are?

WHAT A SELF IS AND WHY YOU THINK YOU HAVE ONE

What We Mean by *Self*

In a memorable passage from chapter 6 of *Introduction to the Middle Way* (*Madhyamakāvatāra*), Candrakīrti (c. 600–650 CE) introduces us to the target of any critique of the idea of the self. He argues that it is important to keep that target clearly in view, and that it is important not to confuse it with other ideas in the conceptual neighborhood. Candrakīrti tells the story of a man who is afraid that a poisonous snake has taken up residence in one of the walls of his house. In order to alleviate his fear, the man searches the house for an elephant, and satisfies himself that there is none there. He then rests at ease. [6.141][1]

What is the moral of this odd Indian tale? Candrakīrti's idea is that even once we recognize that a conception or a commitment is causing us problems, it is often easier and more tempting to confuse it with another idea, to refute that other idea, and to leave the problematic conception in place. This is particularly true when we suffer from an irresistible compulsion to adhere

This is really a book about ethics

to the initial problematic commitment, despite the difficulties it raises. The serpent in this analogy is the self. Candrakīrti thinks that even a little philosophical reflection will convince us that there is something amiss in our thinking that we are *selves.*

Candrakīrti also thinks that the self illusion undermines any attempt to understand who and what we are, and that this failure to understand the nature of our own existence and identity can be devastating to our moral lives. I agree. For this reason, although the majority of this book is concerned with investigating the illusion of the self and defending the idea that we are selfless persons, in the end it is really a book about ethics. I ask the reader to bear this in mind, and I promise that even though I may lead you through some thorny philosophical patches, the payoff will come when we return to ethical reflection in chapters 6–9.

Candrakīrti argues that, despite our ability to understand the incoherence of the idea of the self, we have an innate tendency to think of ourselves as selves. For this reason, he takes it that it is easier to respond to the philosophical unease arising from the self idea by rejecting some other position—such as that the self is the body, or the mind, or even the mind-body complex—than to reject the self entirely. When we do this, we may reassure ourselves that none of these elephants are around, but we leave the serpent in place in our conceptual scheme. So, he argues, the first thing we must do is identify what this self is supposed to be. We thereby ensure that our analyses are directed at the correct target.[2]

I agree. Candrakīrti was writing in an Indian context. So, the view of the self that he took as the object of negation in his argument (an argument we will explore in chapter 2) is the view that to be a sentient being is to be an *ātman.* This term is usually and appropriately translated into English as *self* or *soul.* The idea that the *ātman* lies at the core of our being is ubiquitous in orthodox Indian philosophy, and it was a principal target of Buddhist critique. In the Vedas, and in particular, the Upaniṣads—the texts that ground many of the orthodox Indian philosophical schools—it is characterized as unitary, as the witness of all that we perceive, as the agent of our actions, and as the enjoyer of our aesthetic experience. It is regarded as that which is always the subject, never the object; and as that which persists through life despite changes in body and mind, and which even persists beyond death and in transmigration.[3]

The Indian classic *Bhagavad Gītā* (*Song of the Lord*) characterizes the relation between the self and the embodied person as akin to that between you and your wardrobe. Each day you might put on a new set of clothes, but you are still you, the bearer of those clothes; you are not in any sense identical to them, and you are the same individual who put on different clothes yesterday and who may put on new ones tomorrow. Just so, according to the *Gītā*, you, the *ātman*, put on a new mind and body in each life, but are never identical to any mind or body; instead, you are the *bearer* of that mind and body, which are just as much objects to your subjectivity as any external phenomenon. [2.22][4] Your mind and body are instruments by means of which you know and act on the world, and they are therefore distinct from that self that makes use of those instruments.

Later Indian philosophers such as Uddyotakara (c. sixth century CE) and Śaṅkara (c. eighth century CE) present more systematic accounts of and arguments for the reality of the *ātman*. They argue that it is necessary in order to explain sensory integration, as in seeing the various colors in a butterfly's wings as constituting its variegation, or in assigning sounds, colors, smells, and other such properties to the same object. Without a self, they argue, these would simply be independent sensory experiences, with no common subject, and so could not be assigned to any common object.

They also argue that the self is necessary in order to explain the possibility of memory: my remembering today what I did yesterday requires that the subject of the remembered experience and the subject of the memory are identical. Moreover, they argue that it is necessary in order to account for moral desert, since the one who is to be praised or blamed for any action must be identical to the agent of that action. Our minds and bodies, they concede, change from day to day, violating the condition of identity. So, neither mind nor body, they conclude, is a candidate for the self; the self must be something that stands behind both mind and body as the locus of our identity. We will return to these arguments in more detail in chapter 4.

It is against the existence of this *ātman* that Candrakīrti's arguments are directed. And so, as we shall see when we turn to those arguments, the Buddhist position, and indeed any no-self position, must assume the burden of explaining both the apparent integration of consciousness at each moment and our perceived identity over time in the absence of a unitary subject and agent. In order to be successful, these no-self positions must show both that the idea of the self is incoherent and that everything that the self is meant to explain can be explained in its absence. That is, the proponent of the no-self view must show that everything that the self is meant to explain can actually be accomplished by a *person,* a socially embedded human being with no self.

The *ātman* reemerges in another guise in a Christian context as the *psyche,* another term usually translated as *soul.* In this context as well, the soul is held to be enduring, and to endure even after death (although in the Christian tradition, not through reincarnation, but instead through eternal reward in Heaven or damnation in Hell). The *psyche,* like the *ātman,* is held to be distinct from and to be the possessor of the mind and body; the subject of knowledge; the agent of action; the object of moral approbation or disapprobation; and the enjoyer or sufferer of reward and punishment. Once again, philosophers worked assiduously to develop arguments for the existence and nature of this thing deemed so necessary by religious figures, defending its immortality, its simplicity, and its function as the unitary focus of experience and action. St. Augustine (354–430) also argues that it is immediately available to us in introspection and that it has the distinctive property of *freedom,* of exemption from causation in its active role, a property he deems necessary for moral responsibility.

Those, like Hume and the German philosopher Martin Heidegger (1889–1976),[5] who argue in the Western tradition against the existence of the self, have this Christian version in mind as their target. For our purposes, the Indian *ātman* and the Christian *psyche* are close enough in content, and are defended on similar enough grounds, that we can often treat them as manifestations of the same broad idea. I would add that the difference between a religious view according to which we are reborn and one in which the afterlife is in Heaven or Hell is incidental, and indeed that the entire question of post-mortem existence is irrelevant to the debate about the existence of the self, despite the religious context in which that that debate is often prosecuted, and despite the fact that anxiety about post-mortem existence may motivate our belief in the self.

As we will see, this debate can be, and often is, pursued in an entirely secular register. You might think the fact that the idea that our existence involves the reality of a self emerges in diverse traditions is evidence for its correctness. I hope instead to show you that this ubiquity is in fact evidence for a kind of innate tendency to succumb to a particular cognitive illusion. I hope also to show you that philosophical arguments for the reality of the self are only ways to ramify that illusion into explicit doctrine. And throughout this study, I will use the word *self* only to refer to this kind of self, reserving the word *person* to denote the complex, constructed, socially embedded psychophysical complexes in which I will argue we really consist. This is important: sometimes people use the word *self* indifferently to refer to a self or to a person. If we are careful about the use of these terms, we can avoid confusion as well as the tendency to confuse merely verbal differences with real disagreements.[6]

The efflorescence in the West of systematic argument for the existence of the self and of reflection on its nature (as well as for critique of that idea, to which we return in chapter 2) was the seventeenth- and eighteenth-century period known as the Early Modern period of Western philosophy. Descartes (1596–1650) famously argues in his *Meditations on First Philosophy* that we can be certain of our existence as *res cogitans*, or as *thinking things,* identical not with our bodies, or our perceptual faculties, but with our faculty of abstract reason. Immanuel Kant (1724–1804), defending a position very much like that of many of the orthodox Indian schools, argues in the *Critique of Pure Reason* that the self is a *noumenon,* a transcendental object existing outside of space and time, a pure subject or perceptual, conceptual, and aesthetic experience and agent of action, transcendentally free of the causal order.

The arguments and views of each of these philosophers have been addressed in detail by many scholars, and it is not my purpose here either to articulate or to criticize them (although we will return to them in chapter 4), but only to use them to get a fix on the object of negation, to identify the self the existence of which will be the target of the arguments to come. And the first thing to say is that, like the white whale, belief in the self is ubiquitous: it seems to crop up in some form in every major religious and philosophical tradition. We seem to be wired to experience ourselves *as selves* just as we are wired to see the two lines in the Müller-Lyer illusion as unequal in length, even when we know them to be equal.

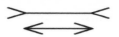

That You Really Believe That You Have Such a Self

"But wait," you might say, "long-dead religious philosophers might have thought that there was such a thing as a self, but I am a modern person. I think no such thing. I take myself to be nothing more than a psychophysical complex, what you, Garfield, want to call a *person*." This is a common reaction, and if it were correct, I would indeed be attacking a straw man. So, I now want to convince you that you, just like the orthodox Indian philosophers, just like the Church Fathers, and just like Descartes and Kant, understand your own identity as that of a *self.* I will do that by means of an easy thought experiment.

One nice thing about imagination and desire is that we can imagine or desire anything, including that which is impossible. When I was very young, I wanted to count to the highest number, but of course there is none; the natural numbers just keep going on and on. The great mathematician David Hilbert (1862–1943) wanted to prove the completeness and consistency of arithmetic, something Kurt Gödel (1906–1978) showed to be impossible. We might wish to live in the universes depicted by the artist of the impossible M. C. Escher (1898–1972). And so on. I say this, because I am going to invite you to imagine, and even to desire, something that might be impossible, and I do not want your sense that it is impossible to lead you to balk in following me in this thought experiment.

The experiment proceeds in two parts. First, think of somebody whose body you would like to inhabit, maybe for a long time, maybe only for a short while. I won't ask you for the details, or for what motivates your choice. Some things are better left private. But just to get the imaginative ball rolling, I will tell you whose body I would like to have: Usain Bolt's (in his racing prime). I only want it for 9.6 seconds. I want to feel what it is like to run that fast. Now, in developing this desire, I do not want to *be* Usain Bolt. Usain Bolt has already achieved that, and it does me no good. I want to be *me, Jay,* with Usain Bolt's body, so that I can enjoy what Usain Bolt experiences.

The very fact that I can formulate this desire or take this leap of the imagination shows me that, deep down—whether correctly or incorrectly—I do not consider myself to be identical to my body, but rather to be something that *has* this body, and that could in principle have another one. Once again, the possible incoherence of this desire or leap of imagination is beside the point: we know that we are capable of desiring, and even imagining, impossible things. In the present argument, I do not take it that it follows from these desires or imaginations that I *am* distinct from my body, any more than I think that my childish desire to count to the highest number demonstrated that there *is* a highest number. Instead, I take the possibility of my forming this desire to show that I *take myself,* at least pre-reflectively, to be a self that is distinct from my body, just as my childish desire showed that *then* I took there to be a highest number.

Now for the second part: we can perform the same exercise with respect to our minds. Imagine somebody whose mind you would like to have, just for a little bit. Once again, whether this desire or act of imagination is coherent or not is beside the point. I'll reveal my desire again. I would love to have Stephen Hawking's mind for long enough to understand general relativity and quantum gravity, but once again, this is not a desire to *be* Stephen Hawking, but to be *me*, enjoying his mind. When you develop this desire, you do not wish to become that other person. Somebody else was already that other person, and that does nothing for you. You want to be *you*, with their mind. And, just as in the case of the body, the very possibility of formulating this desire, or imagining this situation shows that—correctly or incorrectly—you do not consider yourself to *be* your mind, but rather to be something that *has* that mind.

The point of these exercises is neither to argue that there *is* a self nor to argue that there is *not* one. No thought experiment could settle that question; that will be the burden of the subsequent chapters. Instead, I remind you, it is to do two very specific things. First, it allows us to identify what we mean when we talk about a *self*, to identify what will be my object of negation in this study. Second, it is meant to convince you that the view that there is a self is no straw man. That is, I hope that it shows you that you, like nearly everyone, are convinced, deep down, that there is a self, and that this is true even if you, like me, ultimately think that this conviction is false or even incoherent.

Moreover, the very fact that you were able to follow me in this thought experiment shows that, at least before you think hard about it, you take yourself to be distinct from both your mind and your body, to be the thing that *has* your mind and your body, but that, without losing its identity, could take on another mind, another body, just like changing your clothes. The philosopher Jonardon Ganeri correctly emphasizes that when we deny that there is a self in this sense, we are *not* re-identifying the self with the body and the mind (there is no self; just a body, or just a mind); nor are we saying that the self really is the mind-body complex. We are denying that *anything* answers to the definition of a self.[7]

Why We Think We Have a Self

Before we go any further, we might well ask why most of us have this primal conviction that we are selves. Is this conviction the result of careful reflection, or is its origin more primitive than that?

The Tibetan philosopher Tsongkhapa (1357–1419) points out that while some people are convinced of this position philosophically, philosophy cannot be the origin of this belief for two reasons. First, he notes, most people are not philosophers, and have never even reflected on this question. Nonetheless, they still believe that they are selves in the deep sense illuminated by our thought experiments of a moment ago.[8] Even if they do not entertain this idea explicitly, it operates as a background self-understanding that informs their lives. It therefore appears that philosophical conceptions of the self arise from, rather than give rise to, the sense of self.

The second reason that philosophy can't be the origin of the belief in the self, Tsongkhapa argues, is that even philosophers who are convinced through philosophical argument that there is no self—as I am, and as I hope that you will soon be—do not escape this atavistic sense of being a self. And it is worth emphasizing that our instinctive sense of self that enables us to imagine having another body or another mind and these philosophical defenses of the reality of the self address one and the same self. Philosophy, in this case, is trying to make sense of our intuitions, not substituting a "philosophical" self for an "intuitive" one.[9]

Are autobiographers more likely to experience themselves as selves when they're writing autobiography?

For this reason, I suspect that the explanation of the self illusion is not cognitive, but is instead emotional, or even simply biological. There may be good evolutionary explanations of its origin, just as there are almost certainly good evolutionary explanations of how our visual system evolved to succumb to the Müller-Lyer illusion. Each of these may be, as the evolutionary biologist Stephen Jay Gould called them, spandrels, or byproducts, of traits that have real survival value, even if being duped by these illusions has no survival value in itself. But such speculations are well beyond the scope of this book. I would guess that the self illusion arises from a confluence of biological and social causes, but its origin is less important than what motivates our present belief in the self.

The ninth-century Indian philosopher Śāntideva argues in *How to Lead an Awakened Life* (*Bodhicāryāvatāra*) that our conviction that we are selves arises from a primal fear of death, and that we construct the idea of a self as a bulwark against that fear.[10] Śāntideva also argues that the idea that we are selves arises primarily in emotionally charged situations, as when we perceive that we have been harmed, or when pride is aroused. It is then that we think not of our minds or bodies, but of we who possess those minds and bodies. David Hume adopts a similar view. He argues that the thought that we are selves is a product of the passions—that we posit the self as the object of pride and humility, and then reify it in thought.[11] If anything like these analyses is right, the idea of self is grounded not in reason or perception, but in affect.

I find the view that affect is the origin of our sense of self plausible, though perhaps not directly demonstrable. This idea in turn suggests that the universal or near universal drive to posit a self is instinctive, built into our nature as human beings. That fact—if indeed it *is* a fact—would be an *explanation*, but not a *justification* of the view that we are selves. It would be, like the explanations of why we are susceptible to perceptual illusions, an explanation of our tendency to error, not a proof that what we think we see is real. But, once again, to explain the origin of the psychological processes that generate this illusion, and to explain how those processes actually give rise to the conviction that we are selves, we would have to turn to psychology, to biology, and to the social sciences.

In the next few chapters, I will present reasons to think that we are not selves. I take this task to be important, and not simply an abstract metaphysical inquiry. This is because the self illusion *matters*. It matters in part because it obscures our own identities from us, leading to a profound misunderstanding of who and what we are, and of the degree to which our own identities and existence are bound up with those of others. And it matters because it generates a perverse moral vision that engenders an instinctive attitude of self-interest and egoism that none of us can rationally endorse, and from which we would happily free ourselves.

In chapters 6–10 of this book, we will address these important consequences of the self illusion, and we will consider what it would be like to experience ourselves, others, and our world free of that illusion and of its pernicious consequences. I hope that by coming to liberate ourselves from the self illusion, we can lead better, happier lives, and I undertake this investigation guided by that hope.

2

Why You Have No Self

THE VIEW FROM BUDDHISM, PHILOSOPHY, AND SCIENCE

NOW THAT we have some sense of what the target of our analyses is, I want to introduce the basic arguments against the reality of any self. I am going to begin with Indian Buddhist arguments, and then will turn to David Hume's analysis, before concluding with some observations drawn from contemporary neuroscience.

Buddhist Arguments

Perhaps the best-known argument from Buddhist literature against the existence of the self is that found in *The Questions of King Milinda* (*Milindapañha*).[1] The argument is analogical, exploiting a pair of analogies—that of the chariot, and that of the flame. The dialogue has two protagonists: the King (probably based on the Greco-Indian Bactrian king Menander, c. second century BCE) and the (possibly fictional) monk Nāgasena. In the story, Nāgasena has been invited to the Court for a philosophical discussion.

The discussion begins with the King asking the apparently innocent question, "Who are you?" Nāgasena replies coyly that he is really nobody; that he is called *Nāgasena*, but that this is just a name, a designation, and there is nothing to which it really refers. The name *Nāgasena* refers not to his body, his mind, his experiences, nor to anything apart from these. If you seek the referent of the name, he argues, you find nothing. This is a pretty standard articulation of the Buddhist view that there is no self, no *ātman*. But it is just the opening move in the debate.

The King replies that it seems to follow that there is nobody to whom to offer alms, nobody who wears the monastic robe, nobody talking to him, and even nobody denying that he has a self. This appears to be an absurd conclusion, and one that undermines even the ability to assert the position: one can hardly at the same time speak and deny that anyone is speaking. So, the King concludes, there must be something to which the name *Nāgasena* refers, something that presumably constitutes his self. It is at this point that Nāgasena introduces the first of the two central examples in this portion of the dialogue, that of the chariot.

Nāgasena asks the King to consider the chariot on which he rode to the site of the dialogue. The King grants that he did ride a chariot, and so that the chariot he rode exists. But what, Nāgasena asks, is that chariot, really? He points out that the chariot is neither identical to its wheels, nor to its axles, nor to its poles, and so on. It cannot, he argues, be identical to any of its parts, for that would be to leave some others out; to select one part as the *real* chariot would be arbitrary, as well as clearly false. So, he invites the King to conclude, it must be possible for there to be real chariots despite the fact that there is nothing to which *this chariot* refers.

One might be tempted to reply at this point that while the chariot is obviously not identical to any *one* of its parts, or even any proper subset of its parts, it is to be identified with *all* of its parts taken together. But Nāgasena immediately points out to the King that the chariot cannot simply be the sum of those pieces. After all, a pile of chariot pieces on the ground, delivered fresh from the chariot factory, but not yet assembled, is not a chariot. (Anyone who has ordered anything billed as "easy to assemble" will recognize this fact!) But might it be identical to all of those parts suitably arranged, or put together?

"No," says Nāgasena. If it were, then if we changed one of those parts, or changed their arrangement, we would have a different chariot. But that can't be right. We could replace a wheel or an axle, and we would still have the same chariot, saying truly, "I have owned this chariot for years; all I need to do is to replace the wheels every so often," or, "Hey! I just got a new seat for my chariot. Come check it out." We don't say in these cases that we traded the old chariot for a new one; so, a chariot can survive change in its parts, and even disassembly and reassembly. It is therefore neither identical with the collection of its parts, nor with those parts arranged in some particular way.

Nor is the chariot something different from those parts. After all, no chariot as the bearer of those parts remains when they are all removed. For this reason, we cannot think of it as a separate entity that possesses those parts (as we saw in the previous chapter, we are tempted to think of ourselves as possessors of bodies and minds). Nor can we think of it as some mysterious entity located in the parts, but identical with none of them. Nobody takes that possibility seriously. So, Nāgasena argues, the words "the King's chariot" are merely a designation with no determinate referent.

Mode of existence — conventional (handwritten)

But this is not, Nāgasena emphasizes, an argument against the *existence* of the chariot. After all, we began by granting its reality. Instead, the author of the dialogue suggests, while the chariot exists, it does not exist as some singular entity that is either identical to or distinct from its parts. Its mode of existence is merely *conventional*, determined by our customs regarding the application of words like *this chariot*. A complete inventory of the basic constituents of the world, even if it contains chariot parts, contains no chariots.

And this, Nāgasena instructs the King, is how we should think of the *person* who is called Nāgasena and his relation to that name. He is no singular entity. He is neither identical to nor distinct from his parts. He is not the possessor of those parts. There is no single part with which he is identical. His existence is merely nominal. A final account of the basic constituents of the world, even were it to contain his hair, fingers, desires, and experiences, contains no Nāgasena. The self to which the King, as well as the reader of the dialogue, might have thought that the name *Nāgasena* refers is therefore nowhere in the picture. But note that in presenting the analogy of the chariot, we never drew the conclusion that the chariot does not *exist*, or that it was incapable of bearing the King to the site of the debate. Likewise, we have not questioned *whether* Nāgasena exists, but only his *mode* of existence. He does not exist in the *way* we might have imagined him to exist before we considered the matter with care.

Despite the fact that Nāgasena's argument is not meant to call our existence into question, it is unsettling. To say that a *chariot* exists only conventionally is one thing. Conventional existence might be acceptable for mere artifacts. But this analysis might seem to give too little reality to *us*. That is, it might not put to rest the specter of nihilism, the absurd suggestion that neither Nāgasena, nor you, nor I actually exist in the full sense of that term. This is because when we consider our own case, conventional existence doesn't feel like *real* existence, the kind of existence that a *self* is supposed to have. The affect, or the instinct, that leads us to posit the self also leads us to the conviction that we exist in some sense more robust than the conventional reality that persons enjoy.

What, we might ask, is the status of the person who is no self? In particular, one might wonder, what accounts for the continuity of consciousness from one moment to the next, and the persistence of our identity through all of the changes we undergo in our lives if there is no self? Wouldn't we exist even if there were no conventions? Isn't our existence the *precondition* of any conventions? That is, we might ask, what exactly is the mode of existence that persons like us in fact enjoy?[2]

The second principal example is introduced to elucidate that mode of existence a bit further. The King poses this question in terms of rebirth, presupposing the cycle of rebirths taken by classical Indian Buddhists to constitute the world of cyclic existence. He asks what—if there is no self to which *Nāgasena* refers—proceeds from life to life when one is reborn. This makes sense as a way of framing the question in a classical Indian context in which rebirth was taken for granted as a reality, and you might think that this means that the debate makes no contact with our present context. But rebirth *per se* actually has nothing to do with it, and the question and its answer can make perfect sense to us.

The question, and the answer, concern continuity: the problem posed by the King, as well as the solution proffered by Nāgasena, pertain to any identity over time. If we are not selves, the King might as well have asked, what makes me the same individual now that I was when I was a small child, or even ten minutes ago, and that I will be when I am a much older man, or even ten minutes from now? There must be something that makes my subsequent stages all stages of *me,* and your subsequent stages all stages of *you.* Any account of personal identity must explain how and why we persist over time. A self would seem to do that; in its absence, we need an alternative account.

Before we turn to the answer to the King's question, we should reflect for a moment on its complexity. There are two issues here. The first concerns what accounts for my sense that I am the same person now that I was ten minutes ago, and that when I plan to do something in ten minutes, it will be me who does it. That question involves asking why the stages of me are all stages of *me,* and the stages of you are all stages of *you,* and why we never cross over. That is, we must account both for our own identities over time and for our difference from one another. These are questions about *continuity,* or *diachronic identity—identity over time.*

The second issue concerns *synchronic identity,* or *identity at a single time.* We are accustomed to thinking of identity in terms of what Western philosophers call *Leibniz's Law:* identity entails indiscernibility. If two things are different in any respect, they are not identical. Even identical twins are not strictly identical; they are only very *similar.* That is why there are two of them, and not one. Hesperus and Phosphorus however are *identical:* each of those two names denotes the planet Venus. Hesperus and Phosphorus therefore share all of their properties.

Given that I am ten minutes older now than I was ten minutes ago, and will be a further ten minutes older ten minutes from now, these three stages of me differ from one another in at least one respect (age), and certainly more besides (different memories, and even different cells in the body). So, they are not strictly *identical* to one another, but only, like twins, very much *alike.* Since they are not strictly identical, why should we call them stages of the *same* person?

Nāgasena replies to this deceptively complex question by asking the King to reflect on the lamps that are lit in the evening. These small clay lamps then in common use in India did not contain enough oil to last through the night. The practice was to use a nearly depleted lamp to light the next lamp, and so on until daybreak, just as a chain smoker lights the next cigarette using the butt of the previous one.

Now, Nāgasena asks, consider the flame by one's bed that was lit at dusk last night, and the flame to which one awakes this morning. Are they the same, or are they different? Should we say that there was a single flame that burned all night and was transferred from lamp to lamp, or should we say that a sequence of different flames burned through the night, each giving rise to the next? In one obvious sense, the flame of last night and the flame of this morning are different from one another: different oil is being consumed; the flames are burning on distinct clay lamps. But in another equally obvious sense, they are the same: they are each stages of a single causal continuum, an uninterrupted sequence of illumination by florescent gas.[3]

In that sense, we can say truly that the flame lit last night was transferred from lamp to lamp and is still burning this morning. And this identity is neither arbitrary nor promiscuous; it in no way tempts us to identify that flame with all other flames. The flame on our lamp this morning is the same as the one we lit last night; but it is also a different flame than the one burning in a lamp in another room. How, then, we might ask, can we account for its continuity and identity while preserving the difference between the flames in different rooms? It seems like the right thing to say is that the identity and continuity of the flame are constituted in part by causal continuity, in part by common function, but in the end primarily by the fact that we have a convention of talking that way. That is, we conventionally ascribe identity to the elements of such causal sequences, and not to sequences of events that are less causally connected, such as the sequence of lamps in the other room.

This is how *The Questions of King Milinda* invites us to think of our own personal identity. Just as there is no drop of oil or bit of incandescent gas that remains constant in the lamp from evening to morning, there is no self, soul, or ego that persists in me from day to day (let alone from life to life if I believed in rebirth or reincarnation). My body and my psychological states are constantly changing, like the oil and lamps that support the flames. But, like those flames and those lamps, they constitute a causal sequence with a common function. And we have a convention of calling distinct members of such sequences by the same name. So, in one obvious sense, I am not *identical* to the person called by my name yesterday. We are *alike*, causally related, but numerically distinct. In another sense, though, we are the same person. We share a name, many properties, a causal history, and a social role; and that, while not involving a self, is enough.[4]

This pair of analogies is meant to show that we can make sense both of synchronic identity (the chariot) and diachronic identity (the flame) in the absence of anything like the self in which we instinctively presume ourselves to consist. They illustrate the core of the classical Buddhist understanding of persons in the absence of a self. We are, on this view, causally and cognitively open continua of psychophysical processes. No one of these processes by itself captures who we are; none persist unchanged over time; none are independent of the others. Together, they constitute our conventional identity, an identity we can now see to be very robust indeed. To put this another way, we do not stand over and against the world as isolated subjects;

WHY YOU HAVE NO SELF 21

we do not act on the world as transcendent agents. Instead, we
are embedded in the world as part of an interdependent reality.

In *Introduction to the Middle Way*, Candrakīrti adapts the
chariot metaphor from *The Questions of King Milinda*, and re-
works it slightly into what is called in the Buddhist tradition the
Sevenfold Analysis. [6.120–167] He argues that if there is a self, it
must be either identical to or different from the psychophysical
processes that constitute our lives.[5] If the self were identical to
those processes, it would have to be either identical to one of
them, or to several of them, or to all of them when they are
configured in a particular way. If, instead, the self were different,
it would have to be either something that possesses the processes, or something possessed by the processes, or something
entirely disconnected from the processes, or have some incom-
prehensible relationship to them. I think that we can leave aside
the question of whether this partition is actually exhaustive and
exclusive, as it is traditionally taken to be; it certainly offers us
a good template for thinking about the kinds of relations the
self might have to our psychology.

Candrakīrti argues that none of these seven possibilities
makes any sense. To say that the self is identical to any one set
of processes—physical, perceptual, affective, conscious, etc.—
would be arbitrary, and in any case, we identify equally with
each of these sets. But to say that it is identical to all of them
(like the heap of chariot parts on the floor), he argues, would
be to say that there are many selves, and so to take this option
would be to give up on the unity that the self is meant to confer.
Even if we were to say that the self is identical somehow to the
entire collection of those parts, that unity would remain a mysterious achievement, and too weak a unity to constitute that
which we ascribe to a self. The self, after all, was supposed to be
a single center of consciousness and agency, not a committee.

One might reply that the self is identical to the set of parts only when they are arranged just so, functioning fully as a body-mind complex, and that this assembly provides the requisite unity. This, however, Candrakīrti argues, is to ignore the fact that just as there are many possible configurations of the parts of a chariot, there are many possible configurations of psychophysical processes that can constitute a person (even if not all configurations can do so, just as in the case of a chariot). Most importantly, it is to ignore the fact that for each of us, that configuration is constantly changing. It would follow that our self constantly changes. If that were the case, such a "self" could not explain diachronic identity.

So, to identify the self with multiple processes at any one time would lose the synchronic unity the self was supposed to confer—its integrity at a single moment. But to take this other option—that the self is just those parts in a particular arrangement—would be to forego the diachronic identity, or the identity over time, that the self was supposed to confer. The moral of these two stories is that it is impossible to construct the kind of unity that we believe a self to have, out of a multiplicity of parts. If we are to achieve *e pluribus unum,* that *unum* cannot be a self. The self cannot be identical in any sense to the psychophysical processes that constitute us.

Nor does it make sense to say that the self is *different* from these sets of processes. For when we identify ourselves, or describe ourselves, we describe those very processes. How tall are you? You mention your body. How are you feeling? You mention your sensations. What kind of person are you? You mention your personality traits. If you take all of these away, though, there is nothing left: no bearer, no special entity that we recognize apart from our bodies, minds, and experiences. And when we introspect to find ourselves, all we find are our minds, bodies, and experiences.

When I take myself to be or to have a self, as in the thought experiments in chapter 1, the self I posit is one I can know and recognize; but Candrakīrti reminds me that when I look inside, all I find are psychophysical processes, not some ghostly owner hiding behind the curtains. The self, he therefore infers, is neither identical to nor different from our psychophysical processes. But if it existed as we take a self to exist, it would have to be either identical to them or different from them. So, he concludes, the self does not exist. [6]

Candrakīrti argues that we are not selves, but *persons* (the Sanskrit term is *pudgala*). And the person, he argues, is neither identical to nor different from the psychophysical processes; but unlike the self, which is supposed to be an independently existent entity, there is no reason to believe that a person needs to exist in one of these ways. It is instead a socially constructed designation, posited on the bases of those processes, but not reducible to them (in a sense to be worked out in chapter 3). [7]

Consider, to take another analogy, a dollar. There are lots of ways to have a dollar. You might have a dollar bill, a dollar coin, ten dimes, or an electronic record. Your dollar, however, is neither identical to nor different from any of these ways that it might be instantiated. It isn't identical, because you could swap dimes for paper and still have the same dollar. It is not different, because whether you hand me the paper banknote or the stack of dimes, you have handed me your dollar. The dollar isn't something apart from these. If I lose the paper or the dimes, I have lost the dollar. Nor is the dollar some distinct entity that possesses the dimes or the piece of paper. No account that takes the dollar to exist either as identical to or as different from the medium in which it is instantiated makes any sense at all.

There is nothing mysterious about this, and no weird, *sui generis* mode of existence enjoyed by dollars. Even though a dollar has no independent existence, a dollar does exist: the dollar exists on another plane, subject to different constraints than are pieces of paper, bits of metal, or electronic records. To be sure, it still requires some physical instantiation, and some system in which that instantiation counts as a dollar, but instantiation is not identity. Just so with persons: they require psychophysical instantiations. That is, you need a mind and a body (and perhaps a social context) to be a person.

Nonetheless, just as dollars exist on a different plane from dimes, persons exist on a different plane from minds and bodies. Their identities and properties are subject to different constraints from those that govern the identities and properties of minds and bodies. They are thus neither identical to nor different from their psychophysical instantiations. There is no mystery here, even if it takes a bit to get your head around it.

Some might balk at this analogy, on the grounds that we seem to have a choice about whether or not to construct money, but the construction of selves appears to be unavoidable. But this is somewhat beside the present point. The construction of persons *is* perhaps more "natural," or more socially necessary than the construction of dollars. Societies can do without money (at least up to a certain level of social complexity), but they can't do without mutual recognition as persons. Without this recognition we couldn't construct social orders at all, orders that are necessary to our own survival. This is correct. Nonetheless, despite the fact that it is *necessary* to construct persons, it is also true that what is necessary is that *construction,* not a discovery of preexisting selves.

Śāntideva endorses this analysis in *How to Lead an Awakened Life,* and he draws ethical consequences from it. He argues that the dualism of self and other underlies egocentricity. That egocentricity, in turn, leads to a strong sense of self-identity, which causes us to see ourselves as standing at the center of our own moral universes, and so as objects of special regard. He argues that this dualism derives in turn from self-grasping, from seeing the world in terms of the "I and mine" framework that derives from reifying ourselves as selves. He also argues that this is the source of the illusion that others are independent agents.

That illusion, in turn, he argues, issues in two dysfunctional emotional sets. On the one hand, the attribution of independence leads to anger when others offend or wrong us. On the other hand, the sense that we are the sole authors of our own actions leads to egoistic pride in our own accomplishments. So, he suggests, the self illusion is not only an error regarding our mode of existence, but it is an error with disastrous moral results, disenabling true friendship, care, impartiality, and joy in others' achievements. We will return to this issue in chapter 7.

Humean Arguments

This is how the doctrine of no-self is articulated in an Indian Buddhist context. But this idea has arisen in other philosophical contexts as well. Instead of traveling to classical India, we can travel to eighteenth-century Scotland. In his *Treatise of Human Nature,* David Hume argues not only that we are not selves, but also that we don't even have an *idea* of a self—that when we talk about selves, we are literally talking nonsense.[8]

On Hume's view, we often use words that we think have meanings, but which in fact do not. So, he thinks that when we used the word *self,* we use it in roughly the way I characterized its use in chapter 1, this core that is neither identical with the mind nor with the body, but which *possesses* mind and body. And he thinks that that simply makes no sense whatsoever, hence that the idea that we have or are selves is not even false, it is just gibberish. To wonder about the nature of the self, he thinks, is like talking about round squares and wondering what color they might be.

Hume agrees with Candrakīrti (despite having never heard of him) that the self that people *think* they have in mind is supposed to be one of which they are aware, and one that is taken to be permanent in their existence. He writes:

> There are some philosophers, who imagine that we are every moment intimately conscious of what we call our SELF; that we feel its existence and its continuance in existence; and are certain . . . both of its perfect identity and simplicity. [1.4.6.1]

Nobody, that is, takes the self to be something inaccessible to introspection; instead we take it to be the most immediately given, most certainly real object of our experience. Anything that fails to satisfy this description fails to be a self. And there's the rub: Hume invites us to introspect carefully and honestly. He claims that when we do so, we find sensations, perceptions, affect, cognitive states (all of the collections of phenomena identified by Buddhist philosophers, we might note), but nothing more than that. We don't find a subject or self behind them. A bit later in the section just quoted he says:

> For my part, when I enter most intimately into what I call *myself*, I always stumble on some particular perception or other, of heat or cold, light or shade, love or hatred, pain or pleasure. I never catch *myself* at any time without perception, and never can observe anything but the perception. [1.4.6.3]

Moreover, he points out [1.4.6.2], the collection that we find is not constant, but is always changing. There is nothing permanent in our experience. If this is so, Hume argues, when we use the word *self*, there is nothing to which it refers: we are nothing more than bundles of psychophysical processes—changing from moment to moment—who imagine ourselves to be more than that. Note, once again, this is not the absurd claim that we don't exist, but rather the claim that the *way* we exist—as persons—is not the way that we normally take ourselves to exist—as selves.[9]

Hume offers us a nice analogy: we can imagine a church founded by a small number of congregants. As it grows, new congregants join, others leave or die; some are buried in the churchyard. Ministers succeed one another. The old wooden building becomes too small for the growing congregation, and so it is replaced by a larger stone structure. After a number of decades, we might ask, "Is this the same church that was founded decades ago, or a different one?" [1.4.6.13] The parishioners are different; the minister is different; the bodies in the churchyard are different; the building is different. Nonetheless, since it makes sense to say, "This church is fifty years old," in the most important sense, the church remains the same. So, while it is not some entity *different* from its parishioners, minister, building, etc., nor is it *identical* to them, it exists *conventionally*, and that is enough for it to be a real, functioning church. Once again, just so for persons.

It is worth pausing to reflect on the insights we can glean from these canonical Asian and European arguments against the reality of the self. Hume's and Candrakīrti's arguments are not identical; indeed, their conclusions are even slightly different: Candrakīrti concludes that we have no self, but grants the cogency of the idea of the self; Hume denies even its cogency. Nonetheless, they mine the same philosophical vein. The idea is this: People instinctively regard themselves as selves in a very specific sense: they take themselves to persist through time as numerically identical subjects and agents, distinct from their minds, bodies, experiences, and traits. They do so even though they acknowledge that these minds, bodies, experiences, and traits are constantly changing and that they are only contingently connected to their selves.

This is to say that people reflexively locate their identity not in their psychophysical characteristics, but in this hypostasized self. That is the serpent in the wall, and that is the target of Hume's and Candrakīrti's respective analyses. Neither of these two arguments suggests that we are nonexistent, any more than they suggest that chariots and churches are nonexistent; each instead addresses our *mode of existence*. That is, each suggests that it is irrational to claim that we exist as *selves* while affirming that we exist as *persons*.

The Self as Illusion

Let us go a bit deeper into what commitment to a self involves in order both to appreciate the degree to which this myth structures our intuitive understanding of our mode of being, and to appreciate just how easily it crumbles under analysis. These observations are inspired by reflection on the thought of the Indian Buddhist philosopher Vasubandhu (fourth–fifth century CE), particularly the analysis articulated in his short works *Thirty Verses (Triṃśikākārikā)* and *Treatise on the Three Natures (Trisvabhāvanirdesa)*,[10] but they could just as easily be grounded in the phenomenology of Martin Heidegger or in recent work in contemporary neuroscience.

We have encountered four principle conceptual ingredients to the idea of self: priority, unity, subject-object duality, and agency. That is, a self is meant to have a kind of existence *prior to*, or more fundamental than, that of body and mind; it is meant to be a unitary entity, not a multiplicity; it is that which is the subject of our cognitive objects, and so distinct from them; and it is the agent of action and the locus of responsibility.[11]

In his *Tractatus Logico-Philosophicus*, the Austrian philosopher Ludwig Wittgenstein (1889–1951) presents the relation we instinctively presuppose between the self and the world as analogous to that between the eye and the visual field: we take the self to be a transcendental ground of our experience of the world that is absent in the world we experience. The Vedānta system deploys the similar metaphor of the unseen witness to indicate the *ātman*.[12] Each of these metaphors invites us to see the self as *outside* of the world, and as existing independently of it, but as making it known. Let us examine those aspects of the self illusion a bit more closely.

The self is conceived as primordial. That is, it is understood to exist prior to and independent of the world we experience, and to be unitary. Let me explain. First, when we think of ourselves as selves, we assume that our existence is independent of that of our objects, and that we know ourselves more directly, more clearly, more immediately than we know other objects. That is, when I think of myself as a self, I can imagine that even if the entire world outside of me disappeared, I could remain as a center of subjectivity. I take my self to be the basis of my ability to experience the world, not as a part of that world.

Second, we ascribe unity to ourselves. Indeed, as the contemporary philosopher and psychologist Thomas Metzinger emphasizes—describing the views defended by such classical Indian advocates of the reality of *ātman* as Śaṅkara and Uddyotakara, as well as Kant's argument in the *Critique of Pure Reason* for the transcendental unity of apperception—this unity of the self is what we take to account for the unity of experience.[13] We implicitly think that if we were essentially multiple, or fragmented, our experience would have no unity. But our manifest experience of a unified world seems to us to demand a unified self to which it appears, a self whose unity precedes and makes possible the unity of the world experienced.

This unity of the self, however, also grounds a duality: the duality of subject and object. We experience ourselves as subjects and everything else as objects, with a kind of distance between us and the world we experience. This duality so structures our naïve experience that it is hard to imagine that it is constructed, as opposed to natural. We take ourselves to be to the unseen seer, the reality known immediately in experience, the interior in which the external world is replicated and revealed in perception and in thought.

This may be our natural way of representing our experience, but, as I noted earlier, the fact that it is natural does not mean that it corresponds to the reality of our relation to the remainder of the world. After all, as we have seen, it is perfectly natural for us to be susceptible to illusions. In order to see how illusion might creep in here, it is useful to focus on the alternative image: a nondual model of experience of the kind articulated in different ways by philosophers in the Indian Advaita Vedānta system, by those working in the framework of Yogācāra Buddhism, and by Heidegger in his existential phenomenology.

Let us begin with the object side of the apparent duality, and then work our way back to the subject. We will then reverse the order of analysis to get a more complete picture. When we experience external objects, we naturally take ourselves to perceive them just as they are, our experience functioning as an accurate representation of just what things look, sound, smell, taste, and feel like (unless we suspect sensory distortion for some reason). That is, we either take ourselves to be in direct, unmediated contact with the world as it is, or we take that world to be faithfully reproduced inside our consciousness, in a model that Dennett has aptly called "The Cartesian Theatre."[14]

A moment of reflection tells us that this account of perception and knowledge makes no sense. Perception, as all of us know, involves the transformation of information impinging on our sensory apparatus into neural impulses, and the transmission of those impulses along the sensory nerves to diverse areas of the brain, where further neural activity occurs, together constituting our experience of external objects. None of this is controversial, and I am sure that none of it is news to you. But all of this complex neural activity bears no resemblance to a colored, sonorous, tasty, scratchy, odoriferous world: it is all happening in the dark, in brain matter.

This complex of perceptual processes realized in our nervous systems creates an experience for us. But it cannot do this by somehow transporting external objects and their properties into our skulls. That, to say the least, would be dangerous! Nor does it make any sense to suggest that in perception we simply register properties that objects have independent of our perceptual systems and record them in our brains. To do so, we would somehow have to have access to those properties as they are, independently of being perceived, and then record them in perception, which makes no sense at all. And what would it mean for those properties to have a double existence, both outside and inside of our skulls or minds, as suggested by those who think that we perceive the external world by first perceiving inner qualia, or sense data, and then mapping these inner properties onto the outer world? How would we ever connect those inner properties we experience with outer properties with which we have no contact at all?[15]

The world we experience is instead, as philosophers since Vasubandhu in India and Kant in Europe have recognized, a cognitive construction, and its independence of our sensory and cognitive faculties as a reality to be detected and reproduced in consciousness is an illusion. What we construct in response to the causal interaction with our sense organs depends not only on what impinges on them, but on the kinds of sense organs we have, and the kinds of processing that occurs in our nervous system. Animals with different sensory apparatus, or different cognitive architecture may construct very different lived worlds in response to similar sensory stimulation.

This means that the world we experience is not dually related to us, external to us, and independent, but one that we construct in our ongoing engagement with our environment. Birds and sharks, for instance, are sensitive to magnetic fields of which we are oblivious. Insects and many birds perceive light in the ultraviolet and infrared ranges, giving them a much more colorful world than the one we inhabit. Dogs' worlds reflect their enormous olfactory bulbs and complex noses; theirs is a world of volumes of smell that might also be seen and heard, not of chunks of visible matter that might also be heard or smelled. Each of these worlds is a construction, not a replication of a preexisting reality. None of these worlds has greater claim to reality than any other. So, the world we inhabit—just like the worlds of dogs, birds, and bees—is not a world we *encounter*, but a world in which we participate and which we *co-construct*.[16]

Nor is our subjectivity independent of this construction of a world of objects of awareness. Our subjectivity is not a blank screen or a clear mirror waiting for objects to impinge. It is not a bare awareness or pure subjectivity, waiting for an object to turn up. Instead, subjectivity is always the awareness *of those objects*, including both the objects we experience as external to our minds, such as trees and turtles, and those we experience as internal, such as hopes and headaches. So, our awareness of the objects we encounter—while it might present itself to naïve introspection as the experience of something other, dually related to ourselves—is in fact our nondual embeddedness in a world of which we are a part.

In the same sense, our awareness of our subjective states— while it might present itself to naïve introspection as the experi- ence of something immediately present, dually related to that which is other—is in fact just another aspect of our nondual embeddedness in that world. We participate in the construction of what we regard as external to us, and what is external to us participates in the construction of what we experience as the inner. In sum, the very dichotomy of self and other, inner and outer, is a construction, not a given. Much of our life is struc- tured by the illusion that we just find what we in fact construct; but the fact that this illusion structures so much of our experi- ence does not mean that it is not an illusion.

What and Ken Gula's Madman book

The illusory duality of subject and object is matched by an illusion of agent causation, that is, by the illusion that we are the free, uncaused agents of our actions, acting on the world, but causally unconstrained by it. Once again, a moment's serious reflection tells us that this cannot be the case, as we know that we are physically realized biological organisms in a natural world governed by causal laws. Moreover, freedom of this kind is not even something we would want, as philosophers from Hume to Schopenhauer to Dennett have pointed out: real free- dom is not inconsistent with causation; it demands it.[17]

compatibilism Kant

This is because we are free when our desires and intentions *cause* our behavior, when our desires and intentions are *caused* by our values and beliefs, and so forth. Uncaused action, or ran- dom intentions are not only impossible, but also undesirable. Nonetheless, among the illusions for which we seem to be wired is the Augustinian illusion that our decisions to act are uncaused. This is part of the self illusion, for it reflects the as- sumption that we somehow, at least in part of our being, stand not within but outside of the world, and so are exempt from causal determinism. We will turn to the ethical dimensions of this illusion in chapter 7.

And in the end, it is this last point that ties together these four deep aspects of the illusion that we are selves. At the most basic level, the illusion of a self is the illusion that we stand outside of and against the world. We take ourselves pre-reflectively to be singularities: not participants in the world, but spectators of the world, and agents of actions directed on that world. This is what Wittgenstein's metaphor of the relation of the eye to the visual field captures: the feeling that we as selves are not something in the world, but instead that we are the supramundane necessary conditions of its appearance to us.

Wittgenstein's suggestive metaphor is just another version of what Kant called the *transcendental ego,* the self that stands outside of space and time and which constructs space and time as loci for all of the objects of experience, including the empirical subject we introspect. It is what the Vedānta tradition has in mind when it describes the self as the unseen seer, the enjoyer, the agent, always subject, and never object.[18] In each case, we encounter a sophisticated philosophical elaboration of a cognitive instinct, the instinct to posit the self. Nonetheless, no matter how sophisticated the elaboration, to the degree to which the self we instinctively posit is illusory, each of these philosophical elaborations is nothing more than the elaboration of illusion.

So, while these metaphors indeed capture our natural attitude towards ourselves, and are illuminating ways to make that attitude explicit, the moment we deploy them, we see how hollow and indeed incoherent they are. We know that we are part of the world; we know that we do not stand outside of it; we know that we are not exempt from the natural laws that govern

*we are wired to misunderstand
our own mode of existence*

other objects. That is to say, when we think seriously, we know that we are not the selves we presume that we are when not thinking seriously. To my mind, that natural attitude of taking ourselves to be selves is a symptom of a profound instinct for self-alienation, and is the deepest form of what Buddhist philosophers call *primal confusion*, the root of suffering. We are, that is, wired to misunderstand our own mode of existence.[19]

These insights born of philosophical reflection are confirmed by the best contemporary neuroscience. Neuroscience does not reveal a central ego in the brain that marks who we *are*, as opposed to what we experience or do. There is no single place in the brain where it all "comes together," or where consciousness is seated. Instead, neuroscientists focus on the patterns of activity that enable us to bind our experience into an experienced unity, patterns that allow us to self-identify, and that locate us in a spatiotemporal manifold along with our objects of experience. These processes are widely distributed in the brain, drawing on networks associated with perception, motor control, affect, conation, . . .

While the upshot of these processes, as Metzinger puts it, is an illusion, or a model, of a self,[20] they hardly *constitute* a self any more than *Moby-Dick* brings Captain Ahab into real existence. To think that they do is to confuse the serpent in the wall with the nonexistent elephant in the room. This is because the patterns that the most plausible current neuroscientific models identify involve the large-scale coordination of neural activity connecting widely disparate parts of the brain. These include areas associated with proprioception, interoception, perception, language, motor control, long-term and semantic memory, working memory, and so forth.

Moreover, even if—contrary to what the most current neuroscientific theories tell us (and we must concede that they may be wrong, as this field moves very quickly)—there were a central spot in the brain responsible for coordinating and integrating all of the information circulating in its many networks, this would hardly satisfy the definition of a self. For any such center would itself be internally complex, constantly changing, and hardly the thing with which we identify when we say I. That is, it would only be one more process underlying the construction of the illusion of the self. So, not only does the best neuroscience tell us that there is no such center of our identity, but even if it did, the multiplicity of processes necessary to constitute any such identity means that this would not be a self.

All of this is to say that we are many, not one; we are collections of collections of processes, not unities; we are more like hives than bees in that respect. We are of the world, not over and against it. We are dynamic and constantly changing causally interdependent systems of processes, not independent, enduring objects or agents. We have yet to specify more precisely what we are, but at this stage, I hope to have convinced you that whatever we are, we are not selves. In the next chapter, I will start talking about what we are instead, arguing that once we understand what it is to be a *person* instead of a *self*, we can get a clearer, more plausible, understanding of our own identities.

3

What You Really Are

RECOVERING AND DISCOVERING
THE PERSON

SO, WE ARE NOT SELVES. Does that mean that we do not exist at all, as King Milinda suspected it would? Of course not. That would be madness. And it would be equally mad to claim that we have no subjectivity and no agency at all just because we are not transcendent subjects and are not free from the bonds of the causal nexus. "So," we should now ask, "if we are not selves, what are we?" And if our subjectivity and agency are not relations *between* us and the world, how should we understand them? In short, once we put aside the fantasy version of our self-understanding, how can we create a more realistic sense of who we are?

The key to this more realistic self-understanding lies in the distinction between a *self* as we have characterized it and a *person*.[1] Philosophers in both the Indian and the European traditions who have denied the reality of the former have embraced the reality of the latter. It is easiest to get a feel for this distinction by considering the etymology of the English word *person*.

The term derives from the Latin *persona,* literally denoting a mask of the kind worn in the theatre, and metonymically denoting a *role.* We still find this usage in theatre in the phrase *dramatis personae,* the roles in the drama. To be a person is to play a role; the person you are is constituted by the multiple roles you play, including family roles, professional roles, roles in networks of friends, and political roles.[2] This is why John Locke (1632–1704) says in his *Essay Concerning the Human Understanding* that the concept of a person is a *forensic* or legal concept, not an ontological one.

Think about the difference between a role and an actor playing that role. When Benedict Cumberbatch plays Hamlet, the role of Hamlet is realized on stage. Hamlet—not Cumberbatch—is among the *dramatis personae;* Cumberbatch is instead a member of the cast. And there are truths about Hamlet: he is a Dane; he has a troubled relationship with Ophelia; he wants to expose a murder . . . Cumberbatch has none of these traits. And Hamlet is *not* a British actor, nor was he born in 1976, even though Cumberbatch *is* a British actor born in 1976. Moreover, if Cumberbatch is tired of the role, and it is taken over by Al Yankovic, everything true of Hamlet remains true, and it does *not* become true that he was American and born in California in 1959, even though those things are true of Yankovic. In short, even though Hamlet is entirely fictional—and so there is no fact of the matter regarding precisely where or when he was born, or how tall he is, etc.—he is a *real character,* a *persona,* and there are both truths and falsehoods about him that are independent of any facts about the actor who plays him in any particular production of the play.[3]

Moreover, what makes Hamlet the person he is—what constitutes him as a character—is determined not by facts about the actors who play that role, but by what Shakespeare wrote, and by how his play has been received and discussed in the centuries following its composition. We cannot, for instance, ask what Hamlet was *really* like, outside of the context of the play. There *is* no Hamlet outside of that context, and if the play had never been written, even if Benedict Cumberbatch somehow recited all of those lines on a stage, he would not have been playing Hamlet.

The relationship between a fiction and the characters it creates is thus double-edged, reflecting the curious and often overlooked fact that the words *fact* and *fiction* are cognate, sharing the Latin root *fingere*—to *make*, or to *fashion*. Fictions create facts. And this means *both* that the contents of fiction are *creations*, not mind-independent realities, *and* that nonetheless there is truth and falsity with respect to them, truth and falsity constituted by the very act of their creation.

The point of this analogy is thus that to be a person is to be something like Hamlet, not to be like the actor playing Hamlet. Hamlet requires an actor to be instantiated—to be brought to life on the stage—as well as a literary context and a set of theatrical conventions that enable that instantiation or enlivening. In the same sense, we require bodies and collections of psychophysical processes to bring us to life on the stages in which we fret and strut our particular hours (to mix Shakespearean plays) as well as a social context and set of conventions that enable us to be recognized not merely as live human bodies, but as persons among persons. To the extent that we are single characters over our lifetime, we are, like Hamlet, played by a succession of actors: an infant; a toddler; a schoolchild; finally, with any luck, an elder.

There is at least one important difference between Hamlet and one of us: our lines are not written in advance, and our characters are performed in the context of an improv show, not a scripted play. This is important because independence is at the core of the idea of the self, and as we discard *that* idea, one further myth worth discarding is the myth that we ever stand on our own two feet. Instead, our identity is forged only partly by the actors who perform the roles in which our identities consist: we are not performed by solo actors in a stand-up club, but in a vast improv group including friends, family, colleagues, and fellow citizens. Who we are reflects the way our role fits into this indefinitely large, unbounded human drama.

To be sure, the actors who play us—our psychophysical complexes—have important roles in constituting our identity, and this also distinguishes us from Hamlet. But we cannot forget that our identity is constituted as well by the countless other *dramatis personae* in the play that is our lives, who together bring into existence the context in which our own roles make any sense. This fact should call upon us to rethink our supposed independence. And this can be a wonderful realization: we gain a deeper appreciation towards those who help us to become who we are, and a deeper sense of responsibility to others, when we appreciate our collective roles in constituting one another's identity. The resulting humility, gratitude, and resolve both reflect a deeper understanding of our identities and make us better people.

My reality then, is in important ways like that of Hamlet: it is constructed through a set of interlocking narratives, institutions, and histories. But it is different in that my reality, unlike his, is brought to life and made concrete when it is enacted in a particular body at a particular time. That body changes, and the network of relations and institutions in the context of which I am performed changes. But again, like Hamlet, the role transcends those changes, remaining the same role throughout its history.

That is the sense in which we have a *personal* identity, and it is a very real sense, a fact brought into life through our collective narrative and enactive agency: the *personae* that populate our drama are created, not discovered. Our identity endures through change, however, not because we are entities separate from the institutions, relations, narratives, and embodiment that bring us into existence. On the contrary, it endures precisely because of those very institutions, relations, narratives, and in virtue of that very embodiment.

Nor is the identity that transcends all of that difference constituted by our being identical with those institutions, relations, narratives, and embodiment. Rather it emerges from them, as a conceptual construct that they undergird, but which is neither identical to them nor reducible to them. That is, as Candrakīrti put it, we are neither identical to nor different from the facts that ground our existence. After all, it would be wrong to say that Hamlet is identical to the words in Shakespeare's script, or to the series of performances of his role, or to the critical literature on the play, or even to all of these things put together, just as the chariot in Candrakīrti's deployment is neither identical to any of its parts, nor to their assembly, etc. Hamlet is a fictional Danish prince, not a nonfictional set of texts and practices. No set of texts and practices can fall in love with Ophelia or betray Rosencrantz and Guildenstern. It would be equally wrong to say that Hamlet is *different* from the words, performances, critical literature, etc. For apart from them, there is no Hamlet.[4]

Having reconstructed our identity as the identity of persons, one might think that we have not refuted the reality of the self, but instead effectively reconstructed the self. Why isn't the moral of this story simply that we were wrong initially about the nature of the self—that it is not an essential core, subject, agent, etc., but instead this high-level conceptual construction? That

is, one might ask, are we just involved in a verbal dispute? After
all, one might say, having identified the person, what is the
harm in calling that the self?

This is where it is wise to recall Candrakīrti's serpent. The reason that we care about the self in the first place is that it is what
Buddhist philosophers call "the object of self-grasping," that
which we naïvely take ourselves to be, and which grounds many
of our instinctive affective and moral responses. We saw in chapter 1 that we can identify such a self, and that we do instinctively
regard our own identities as bound up with such a self. And the
self that we instinctively grasp and that plays this deep psychological role is *not* the person we have just characterized. The self
is taken to be preexistent, primordial, unitary, and transcendent
of the world of objects, independent of body, mind, and social
context. The person is constructed; the person is dependent on
the psychophysical and social network in which it is realized; the
person is complex, embodied and embedded. That is the difference between the actor and the role. We are roles, not actors.

By distinguishing the self from the person, we can separate
what we are from what we naïvely take ourselves to be; we can
distinguish the reality of our existence from its appearance. But
more than that, we can come to see just how powerfully cognitive instinct can shape our sense of who and what we are. And
this in turn can dislodge an entire set of seductive myths to
which we also unreflectively subscribe, all myths grounded in
the self illusion. Here are three of the most important, seductive, and pernicious of those myths:

  i) that we know ourselves immediately and infallibly as
     selves;
  ii) that in our capacity as subjects and agents, there is
     something irreducibly special or transcendent about
     our mode of existence;

iii) that the so-called first-person perspective involves a special kind of immediate self-access.

To dispel these myths is philosophical progress. We will see that it gives us a clearer picture of who we are. And as we will see, it can facilitate moral progress as well.

To be sure, the fact that our identity emerges in interdependence on one another does not always work in our favor. While we can celebrate the ways that our loved ones and social structures support us in our growth and aspirations, it is equally true that oppressive social structures or abusive individuals often craft scripts and sculpt characters in deeply harmful ways. This is in part why racism, sexism, gender oppression, income inequality, and structural violence are so devastating at so many levels, destroying even the sense of who we are. Interdependence can thus be a source of misery as well as of joy; of despair as well as of gratitude. This does not, however, mean that we can escape it. Interdependence is a fact of life; and our identity as persons is a consequence of that interdependence, for good and for ill. It is therefore incumbent upon us to think its dimensions, manifestations, and impacts through with care, discernment, and a moral sensibility. This also suggests that when we think about the influence of these social structures on our formation as individuals, it makes more sense to ask the relevant questions about persons than about selves.[5]

4

The Self Strikes Back I

THE TRANSCENDENT SELF

EVEN THOUGH THE ARGUMENTS we considered in the last two chapters may seem entirely convincing, they have not convinced everyone. Indian Buddhists got pushback from their orthodox Indian interlocutors, and contemporary no-self theorists are engaged in debate with proponents of the existence of the self who are influenced by the European phenomenological tradition. Considering these arguments enables us to develop a deeper understanding of what is at stake in such debates. Each of the principal counterarguments figures both in classical Indian and contemporary Western debates about the self.

In this chapter, we will first consider a classic argument for the reality of the self that we find both in early modern Europe and in ancient India. We will then consider a set of transcendental arguments for the existence of the self. In the next chapter, we will consider some contemporary reconceptualizations of what a self might be. This discussion may sometimes get a little bit technical, and it will bring us into direct dialogue with some philosophers who have defended the reality of the self. It may sometimes be hard to see the forest for the trees. But, if we are to get really clear about this issue and to appreciate why those who believe that there is a self are committed to that position, we must follow the most important arguments on each side of the debate. Appreciation of the details enables us to address the ethical and existential implications of our lives as selfless persons in greater depth.

Uddyotakara and Descartes: The Necessity of the Self for Consciousness

There is one quick argument that many have seen as a direct route to proving the reality of the self. We encounter it both in the Indian and European contexts. I call it the *Cartesian* argument, because its best-known Western source is Descartes's *Meditations*. But it occurs much earlier in the work of the Indian philosopher Uddyotakara (seventh century).[1] There is also an Islamic precedent for the argument in Ibn Sena's (980–1038) "flying man" thought experiment.[2] In Descartes's formulation, it is known as the *cogito* argument, abbreviating the dictum that lies at its heart, *Cogito. Ergo sum.* (I think. Therefore, I exist.)

The literature on this argument, and on its role in Descartes's project in the *Meditations*, is vast. Much of the discussion of that argument, however, is beside the present point. For our purposes, it is only relevant to note that while this argument is sometimes taken to demonstrate the reality of the self, it does not succeed in doing so. The argument has a single premise: *Cogito. I am thinking.* Let us first ask what follows from that premise. That premise—*I am thinking*—immediately entails that at the moment when it is asserted, there is thought. Thought, however, is not a self. It therefore does not follow *immediately* that I am a self.

But this is not the end of the story: as we must concede, thought requires a thinker, and perhaps that thinker would have to be a self. Indeed, when Descartes draws the next important conclusion in the chain of argument in which the *Cogito* figures, it is *Sum res cogitans*—*I am a thinking thing*. And that is a reasonable inference (so long as we restrict it—as Descartes does—to the moments when I am in fact thinking, and so long as we don't smuggle in any account of what kind of thing that thinker is). So, the argument *does* demonstrate that Descartes, you, and I are (at least sometimes) thinking things, agents of thought. But that still doesn't get us to the conclusion that we are *selves*, as we don't yet have any reason to believe that agents of thought must be selves. It is therefore necessary, if this argument is to convince us that we have selves, to show that a thinking thing must be a self.

So, in order to show this, Uddyotakara and Descartes each go further. To understand that path onward, we must take a detour into their accounts of what it is to be a thing, or an object. Each account is committed to a fairly common view in classical metaphysics, the view that to be an object is to be a *substance* with *properties*. Let us begin by getting a sense of the intuitive pull of this metaphysical position, and how it is intended to function as a bridge to take us from the idea that we are thinking things to the conclusion that we are selves.

Consider the apple on my desk. It does seem that the apple can't *be* just its roundness, redness, and sweetness; it is, we might think, the thing that *is* round, red, and sweet. That is, one might think that there must be some basic stuff that bears those properties, or in which those properties *inhere* (to use the technical term philosophers use for the relation between substances and their properties). On this view, it seems that when we refer to the apple itself, we don't refer to its properties. Instead, we refer to an enduring base that supports those properties and that acquires other properties as it changes, some*thing* that *is now* round, red, and sweet, but which once was green and sour, and which soon might be squishy and somewhat rotten.

This is the intuition that motivates thinking of objects, including people, as substances with attributes. Uddyotakara and Descartes each argue that thought is a property or an action of a thinking thing, just as redness is a property of my apple. Since properties can only inhere in substances, and actions can only be undertaken by substantial agents, they each conclude that thinkers are substantial agents. And to be such a substantial agent is to be a self—that special kind of substance in which thought inheres, or that performs acts of thought.[3]

So, in this argument, the conclusion that we are substantial selves depends on a bridge, the premise that only *substances* can have properties, perform actions, or maintain their identity through time. To discuss this metaphysical view, what motivates it, and to address everything that is wrong with it, would take us far afield, and we will not go there. But we don't have to: as soon as we spell this idea out, we can see that it will run into insuperable problems. The first and most obvious is that nobody has ever seen such propertyless substance, and it plays no role in any scientific theory. That is, there is no good positive reason to believe that substance is real, or that the substance-attribute way of thinking about apples or persons makes any sense. It is, we might say, little more than a metaphor.

Moreover, as Bishop George Berkeley (1685–1753) argues in his *Three Dialogues between Hylas and Philonous*, there is an easy route to showing the incoherence of this view, as it generates a vicious infinite regress of substances and relations. This is because the supposed inherence relation that connects properties to the substances in which they are meant to inhere is a *relation*, and a relation is a property of a pair of things. For instance, the fact that Talisker is my dog means that he and I are connected by the relation of dog-ownership. Another way to say that is that together, we have the property of dog-and-owner.

Now, if the substance-attribute picture is right, this property inheres in the pair of us. So far, there is no big problem. But here comes the kicker: since *inherence* is a relation between a substance and its properties, it itself must also be a *property*. And this sets up the vicious regress, for then inherence must inhere in yet another substance, and that inherence needs yet another substantial basis, and so on *ad infinitum*. The lack of any scientific evidence for substance is one good methodological reason to reject the substance-attribute picture as unsupported. This regress argument is a second good reason for us to jettison the substance-attribute model of reality, this time on the stronger grounds of incoherence. And if we reject this account of what it is to be a thing, we lose the bridge from the acknowledgment that we are thinking things to the conclusion that we are substances, and so that we are selves. This effectively refutes the Cartesian argument for the reality of the self, as that argument depends on this bridge.

Even if we *granted* the cogency of substance-attribute metaphysics, another central premise of the Cartesian argument is manifestly false, *viz.*, that only substances can act or have properties. Such composite, non-substantial entities as corporations, committees, colleges, and nations have plenty of properties and perform plenty of actions. They may be democracies or monarchies, banks or manufacturers, etc. They also take positions, and do so for reasons: they enact laws, go to war, pay dividends, and grant degrees. And we certainly would not want to say that these composite entities are *substances*, on pain of multiplying substances endlessly, or of rendering the term empty. There is therefore no reason not to believe that composite, non-substantial persons can have properties, such as thinking, as well.

So, while the *cogito* argument and its dialectical kin may demonstrate that we exist—again, at least at certain moments—they do nothing to demonstrate the *kind* of existence we enjoy, and in particular that we are *selves*, as opposed to *persons*. They hence are irrelevant to the question we are addressing. We now set those arguments aside, and turn to some more compelling arguments, each of which also has a long pedigree and each of which is alive and well in contemporary debates about the self.

Transcendental Arguments for the Existence of the Self

Most contemporary arguments for the reality of the self are instances of what Immanuel Kant called a *transcendental argument*. In a transcendental argument, it is taken for granted that some phenomenon (called the *explanandum*—the thing to be explained) is real, and then we argue that something else must be the case (the *explanans*) in order to explain the reality of that phenomenon.[4]

Proponents of the existence of the self who adduce transcendental arguments for its reality (Kant included) argue that the reality of the self is necessary to explain one or all of the following phenomena: (1) the *synchronic* unity of consciousness and of its objects; (2) the *diachronic* unity of personal identity;[5] (3) the *sense of oneself* in agency and subjectivity; (4) the possibility of individuating and distinguishing obviously distinct individual persons. We will consider synchronic and diachronic identity in this chapter. In each case, we will first set out the transcendental argument for the existence of the self as presented by its proponents, and then explain why the argument does not succeed in establishing its intended conclusion. We will consider agency in chapter 7, and individuation in chapter 8.

Before we turn directly to these arguments from synchronic and diachronic identity, we should observe that there are two possible lines of attack against any transcendental argument. On the one hand, one might deny that the purportedly obvious *explanandum* of the argument (the phenomenon that is taken for granted and which needs to be explained) is in fact a reality. One might, for instance, argue that the phenomenon in question has been misdescribed, or that it is simply illusory. Or, on the other hand, one might argue that the purported *explanans* (that which explains the *explanandum*) is not required to explain that phenomenon, that we can explain it in some other way. If either form of attack is successful, the transcendental argument fails to establish its conclusion.

Suppose for instance that someone presented a transcendental argument for the existence of the Abrahamic God based on the perfection of the world. They might begin by noting that the world is a perfect place, with everything just as it should be (the *explanandum*) and then argue that a necessary condition of this perfection is the world's having been created by a divine being (the *explanans*). That is, they point to the wonders of nature, the beauty of roses, the capacities of philosophers to dream up arguments like this, etc., and claim that none of this could have been produced by chance. Just as a beautiful work of art or an accurate watch must be produced by a great artist or a skilled watchmaker, a beautiful, precisely organized world must be produced by a great, skilled creator.[6]

One might reply to this argument in two ways. First, one might argue that the world is not as perfect as it is made out to be (in that it contains a lot of suffering, for instance, or cases of really bad engineering, such as human knees), thus calling the *explanandum* into question. If there is nothing to be explained, there is no need to look for the explanation. This would be to deny the truth of the premise of the argument. Or, one might concede the world's perfection, but argue that although it is perfect, natural, non-divine processes could just as well account for that perfection (such as evolution, or sustained planning by expert committees). This second strategy concedes the premise, and attacks the inference, denying the necessity of the *explanans*. Once again, either strategy, were it to succeed, would derail the argument, leaving the conclusion unsupported. In what follows, we will sometimes adopt one of these strategies, and sometimes the other.

Transcendental Arguments for the Existence of the Self: Synchronic Identity

Let us begin with the phenomenon of synchronic identity. There are two classes of transcendental argument for the existence of the self that take synchronic identity as their *explanandum*. The first, on the subjective side, is what is often called the *argument from the unity of consciousness*. This argument takes as its *explanandum* the apparent fact that our experience seems unified in a common, simple subject, as opposed to a committee of sensory and cognitive subjectivities. The second, on the objective side, concerns what is sometimes called the *unity of the object*.

Let us begin with arguments from the unity of the subject. In classical India, philosophers from both the Nyāya and the Vedānta traditions took the unity of consciousness as simply an obvious fact. They also each argued that this unity is explicable only if we suppose the existence of an *ātman* or self that serves as the subject of all experience. They argued that this self has to be distinct from both mind and body, on the grounds that it is the subject of both physical sensory experience and introspective experience of our own mental states. Since it is the subject of both kinds of experience, and subjects are distinct from their objects, the *ātman,* they argued, can be neither mind nor body.

Moreover, they argued, all of our experiences are present in a single subjectivity. That is, I do not take my visual experience to be experienced by one subject, my auditory experience by another, and my awareness of my puzzlement about the self by yet another. To do so, they argue, would be to take myself to be an in inner committee of multiple subjects, cooperating to know the world. This, they say, would fly in the face of the fact that my experience is so obviously unified, and is all available to *me,* not some of it to each of many strange inner associates. It just seems obvious, they take it, that a single subject—me—is the subject of all of these experiences, and that they all constitute a single inner life. So, they argue, the self must not only be distinct from body and mind, but it must be unitary.

Finally, proponents of this position argue, this unity can only be *apparent* if it is also *real*: that I can't even *think* that my experience is unified unless it really is. Here is how this goes: I obviously experience myself as a cognitive and experiential unity— as a single subject of experience. That fact, they say, leads to two possibilities: either that experience is veridical, and I am such a unity, or it is illusory. But here is the catch: even if it is illusory, the illusion is possible only if there is a single subject to be fooled: that is, even for me to *believe myself* to be unitary, when I am actually manifold, there must be a single *me* who believes in that unity. So, either way, I must be a unitary being. To put this point another way, the appearance of my own unity cannot actually be an illusion. So, since I appear to be a unity, I must be one. And since I am a unity whereas my mind and my body are each complex multiplicities of more basic phenomena, I must be distinct from those. So, they conclude, I am a self.[7] This is the classical Indian version of the argument.

Kant offers a similar argument in the *Transcendental Deduction of the Categories* section of the second edition of the *Critique of Pure Reason*. There he argues that the phrase *I think* must be capable of accompanying any experience or judgment, otherwise that experience would not be experienced as *mine*. That sense of *being mine* is essential, he argues, for anything being experienced at all. Moreover, for it to be possible even to judge that multiple experiences are all *mine*, the referent of the *I* to which each is referred must be the same.

Contemporary phenomenologists often refer to this as the *for-me-ness* of experience, a kind of pre-reflective, unarticulated, implicit, or primordial taking of all outer and inner awareness as *mine* that constitutes a single field of subjectivity.[8] We will return to these formulations in the next chapter. These contemporary philosophers thus follow Kant in taking seriously the intuition that any experience that did not somehow announce itself with a special marker as *my* experience wouldn't be experience at all. That single field of experience, they argue, demands unification by a single subject.

Kant, like many classical Indian Orthodox philosophers, including those from the Nyāya, Mīmāṃsā, and Vedānta traditions, takes this unifying self to be a *transcendental ego*, or a pure subject that is never an object of experience. Many of Kant's own reasons for this are complex and beyond the scope of this discussion. But one reason is that Kant argues that space and time are projected by the self as loci for objects. This is because to experience anything as an object is to experience it *in* space and time; we can't imagine a non-spatiotemporal object. So, he concludes, space and time are not themselves objects among other objects, but rather *the way we experience* all objects, structures that we must presuppose in order to experience anything as an object.

But the self, Kant claims, is essentially a *subject,* and so it cannot be an object. And he concludes from this that while all objects are found in space and time, the transcendental ego lies outside of space and time as their precondition. This transcendental ego is different from what he calls the *empirical ego*—the mind we know when we engage in introspection—and from anything physical, since both inner and outer objects of experience are found in time, and outer ones in space as well. The transcendental ego therefore has a mode of being entirely distinct from its objects, and so distinct from any spatiotemporally located *person.* It functions as the ground of our awareness not only of the external world but also of our own existence as cognitive agents, and so, once again, the transcendental ego must be distinct from our physical or psychological manifestations.

Note that this account of the transcendental ego, and the arguments for its reality, accord with the way we characterized the self in chapter 1. It is neither mind nor body, but that which *has* a mind and a body; it is always subject or agent, and never object. It is thus clear that these are arguments for the existence of the very kind of self with which we are concerned in this investigation. This is not accidental. For, as we just noted, both mind and body are complex entities; neither is experienced as simple, and neither is a plausible seat of unified experience. Moreover, mind and body can each be taken as an object in introspection, interoception, or proprioception. Therefore, these proponents of the reality of the self argue, neither mind nor body is that with which we identify when we use the first-person pronoun to denote the *subject* that experiences them as *its* mind and body.

These arguments thus begin with the idea that we identify with something in the *subject* side of experience, not anything on the *object* side. And, these proponents of a transcendental ego or *ātman* argue, something simple is needed on that side to unify the manifold of our experience. For everything I experience is, by definition—and this is the premise of the transcendental argument—experienced *as mine,* in a single field of reality, not as disconnected experiences that might belong to different subjects. If this is so (and this is the inference in this transcendental argument), there must be a single consciousness to which they all appear. This is the *self.* Kant and his followers, we might say, are only making much more precise and systematic the basic, instinctive intuition of the reality of the self that we explored in chapter 1.

This is the transcendental argument for the reality of the self from the subjective side. We will return to these arguments shortly to see how, despite how plausible they may sound, they fail to establish the reality of the self. But, as Uddyotakara in India and Kant in Prussia each also pointed out, a similar argument can be mounted from the side of the object. Not only is there a problem to be solved about the unity of the subjective field of experience, but there is a problem regarding how individual objects that we experience are unified.[9]

This second group of arguments raise what is called in cognitive science the *binding problem,* the puzzle of how we bind properties together as properties of single objects, taking an egg to be oval and white and an apple to be round and red, but never, when gazing at an egg and an apple, attaching the roundness to the egg or the whiteness to the apple. When we consider our experience from this side, we ask what could unify the various features of the objects we experience—shape, color, sound, smell, etc.—into a single object of experience. In each case, those who advance these arguments claim that only a self could explain the manifest unity in question.

To take Uddyotakara's example, if I watch a person dancing, I experience color, shape, sound, perhaps smell, and texture if I am close enough, and I am aware of all of this changing over time. I may also experience different kinds of affective responses to the dance, such as anticipation, pleasure, and disappointment when it is all over. I do not, however, experience these as disjointed sensations—a bit of movement, a bit of color, a bit of pleasure—but rather as properties of a single object or event extended and articulated in space and time. That is, I *bind* all of these sensations and affective responses to experience them as properties of a unified object of experience.

Just as the unity of the *subject* was the key premise of the transcendental argument we just discussed, the unity of the *object* is the premise of the second kind of transcendental argument. The inference is then straightforward: For all of these multiple and distinct properties to be bound to a single object requires that they all be represented by a single subject. If they were not, one subject might assign a property to one object, and another to another.

Moreover, that single subject can't simply be one or another cognitive state or process. This is so for two reasons. First, even cognitive states and processes get unified in this way, bound to a single cognitive subject in introspection: we do not experience our inner life as fragmented into unrelated parts experienced by different subjects any more than we experience external objects as fragmented. Second, because multiple cognitive states and processes are involved in any such variegated experience, that which binds them must be something beyond those states and processes. So, this argument concludes, there must be a single subject of experience to which all of these properties are present that binds them to a single object. This, the proponent of the argument concludes, is the self.

Each of these arguments, whether from the side of the subject or from the side of the object, is an argument for a *transcendent* self—a self that stands *behind* both mind and body and therefore that is distinct from both. This fact should convince us of two things: first, that we are talking about a *self* here in the sense relevant to this discussion (as opposed to a *person*); second, that something has gone terribly wrong metaphysically.

It should convince us that we are talking about the *self* because it perfectly captures that idea of the subject that stands behind mind and body as their possessor, that to which we seem to be so atavistically attached. That is the self, not the person. It should convince us that something has gone terribly *wrong* because, when we reflect carefully, it does not seem at all plausible that we really exist outside of space and time and distinct from our psychophysical embodiment. This is so despite the fact that *prior* to reflection, as when we fantasize about having someone else's body and mind, that is *exactly* how we imagine ourselves. And the fact that our pre-reflective intuitions and what we know to be the case on reflection are so different should remind us that our instincts and fantasies are not always rational, or good guides to reality. The task of the kind of philosophical reflection in which we are now engaged is often not to *confirm* what we believe intuitively, but to *correct* the errors to which our intuitions are prone.

All of this suggests that something is seriously wrong with all of these transcendental arguments, regardless of how plausible they appear to be. It is now time to see just what goes wrong. So, let us ask, in each case, is it the premise or the inference that is at fault? In these cases, the answer is *both*. For now, we will consider some reasons to be *suspicious* of the premise, suspicions that we will confirm later. We will then turn to the inference, which we will show to be invalid.

Let us first briefly consider the premise that is shared by all of the arguments we have just considered: we are asked to grant that our experience is unified. To be sure, this is superficially plausible; our experience does seem to be unified, at least prior to reflection. But we should be careful here, and not simply assume that our pre-reflective intuitions are correct. After all, that alleged unity has not been proven, and it might well be as illusory as the self that is supposed to be distinct from mind and body.

In order to see that this may be so, let us return, for an analogy, to the case of perception. We know that we are subject to perceptual illusions. For that reason, we would not expect to explain the fact that the lines of the Müller-Lyer illusion (p. 7) *appear* to be unequal in length by demonstrating they *really are* unequal in length. Instead, we would explain it by conceding that they are in fact *equal* in length and then showing how those arrowheads fool our visual system into representing them as unequal. We would be wrong to take the appearance of inequality as a guide to reality, and we would be correct to be suspicious of the accuracy of our own perceptual faculties.

By analogy, since we know that we are subject to cognitive or introspective illusions as well as perceptual illusions, we should not take the fact that the objects of our experience *appear* to be unified to be explained by showing how they *are* unified. It may well be that, as in the Müller-Lyer case, this appearance is to be explained not by its accuracy, but by our susceptibility to an introspective error. We will postpone detailed discussion of this issue for now, but we will return to it in chapter 5. Here, we will show that the transcendental arguments we have been considering fail due to the invalidity of the inference from their premises to the conclusion that there is a self.

So, let us set aside any doubts about this premise, and grant it for a moment, just for the sake of argument. That is, let us suppose that our experience *is* unified at least in our introspective awareness of it, and that the objects we experience *are* bound into propertied unities. Even if we do so, however, we will see that the inference in each of these arguments is invalid. That is, even if we grant the apparent unity of the subject, or of the object, we need not accept the conclusion that this unity can only be explained by the existence of a singular self, let alone by a transcendent self that stands behind all that we experience. We now turn to the critique of the inferential step in these arguments.

First, we should bear in mind that when we talk about the unity of our experience, we are talking about the experience of an *apparent* world, a world as delivered to us by being constructed by our sensory and cognitive faculties in response to sensory stimulation. How does that world arise? Well, light falls on our eyes; chemicals interact with receptors in our nose; fluctuations in air pressure are registered by our ears; etc. These interactions cause impulses to travel up our nerves to our brains, where a cascade of neural processes occurs, resulting in our experience of a world. That experience, as I pointed out in chapter 2, is literally *constructed* by us, not passively received.

That experience—not the external world, which appears to be a collection of multiple entities—is what, according to the proponents of the arguments we have been considering, is unified by a self. So, as we think about the construction of this unified experience, let us consider some apt analogies to this process. A large construction crew can build a single building from multifarious materials, with the entire project in their collective intention, but with no single member cognizant of the entire operation. A congressional committee can produce legislation about which no single member is fully knowledgeable. A college can graduate a student in virtue of the efforts of many faculty and staff members, without any single person surveying all of her accomplishments.

Just so, a plethora of subconscious perceptual and cognitive processes can jointly generate the representation of unitary objects in a unified experiential field. There is no need for their interaction to be integrated or managed in any single neural or cognitive structure. Indeed, this is precisely how the brain appears to work. The fact that the field and the objects in it are experienced in introspection as unified does not entail that this unity is achieved by a unified subject of consciousness, any more than the fact a legislature passes a single bill entails that there is a single legislator, no more than the fact that a student earns a single degree entails that she was taught only by a single teacher. It entails only that there is a set of processes robust and integrated enough to create a single manifold of experience. An *organism* may be necessary for this task, but not a *self*. So, even the unity of experience would not entail the existence of a unified subject of experience; nor does a unified object presuppose a unified subject. This shows that the inferences in both the argument from the unity of the subject and in the argument from the unity of the object fail to establish the reality of the self.[10]

Those who defend the unity of the subject might respond that this reply begs the question, that is, that it assumes the conclusion it is trying to establish. This is because they might say that it presupposes that a disunified subject can have unified experience, which is the very question at issue. Thus, they might argue, we must begin by granting the premise that a unified experiential field can only be the field of a unified self. Since my reply does not grant this, but it presupposes instead that a *disunified* subject can experience a unified objective field, the proponent continues, I have assumed what is to be proven.

We should not be convinced by this dialectical move, however. In replying to the transcendental arguments as I have done, I do not beg the question; instead, it is the proponent of the self who does so. This is because *they* assume without argument that only a unified subject can have unitary experience. I provide examples of cases where complex entities produce single products, showing that this is *possible*. I also point to the complexity of the central nervous system to show that this analogy is *plausible*. And we can thus see that the assumption by the proponent of the self that only a unified subject could have unified experience is not an innocent assumption, simply because we have examples of disunified agents that produce unified products: a unified building does not presuppose a unified builder, nor does a single act of Congress presuppose a single legislator as its author, nor does a single graduate presuppose a single teacher. So, a unified field of experience cannot be assumed to presuppose a self. That field can emerge from the cooperation of a multiplicity of cognitive functions, and most likely does. To get from unity to the self requires an argument that *only* a unitary self could accomplish the task, and this has not been proven. It is hence the *proponent* of this argument, not the critic, who assumes that which is to be proven.

The contemporary philosopher-psychologist Thomas Metzinger defends the position I am urging. He argues that our cognitive architecture reflexively creates what he calls a *phenomenal self model*, that is, a complex representation of a self. That model includes representations of our body, of our current sensory state, of our cognitive processes, and of our orientation to the world, as well as representations of our relation to the past and the future. It represents us as agents, as centers of experience, and as extended in time and in space. And this representation induces a first-person perspective on our experience through our identification with it. That model may have some value: it may help us to orient ourselves in space and time, for instance.[11]

Nonetheless, Metzinger emphasizes, while these cognitive processes give us a *sense of self*, and while they create a perspective from which that self appears to be the center or locus of our experience and agency, the representation is *false*. It constitutes an illusion.[12] That is, we cannot infer from a sense of self to the reality of a self; and we cannot infer from the fact that a unity is presented to us that that unity is real. So much for arguments for the reality of the self that are based on *synchronic* unity. Even if we grant their crucial premises (and, once again, a bit later we will call even those premises into question), their conclusion simply does not follow.

Transcendental Arguments for the Existence of the Self: Diachronic Identity

But even if we grant that the experience of *synchronic* unity can be achieved by a set of selfless interlocking perceptual and cognitive processes, one might argue that *diachronic* unity presupposes more than that. We will now consider another argument—familiar in both Indian and Western philosophy.[13] Stripped of the details that distinguish the various versions in which it appears, it goes like this: We experience ourselves as extended over time, as having existed in the past, as continuing as the same being now, and as (hopefully) continuing to exist in the future. If we were not aware of ourselves as extended over time, this argument continues, we could not be aware of ourselves as existent at all. This is because even to be aware of oneself as existing at a moment of time requires one to think of that moment in relation to other moments of time at which one existed. That is, to experience myself as existing *now* is to experience myself as existing at *this* moment, which is later than *another* moment at which I existed, and prior to another in which I may exist.

Our experience of the present hence includes our memories of past times and our anticipation of future times, as times already experienced or as times to be experienced by *me*. If it did not, it would not even be the experience of the *present*, since that only makes sense in relation to the past and the future. Therefore, the proponent of this kind of argument concludes, for me to have any experience at all, I must endure over time; that thing that endures over time, moreover, must be a self.

Moreover, this argument continues, if I were nothing but a succession, with no endurance over time, then memory would be impossible. This is because the subject I am now could not have existed in the past. And so when I take myself to be remembering, the experience I take myself to remember would be that of somebody else. That isn't memory: to remember something, I myself would have had to experience it. And on the succession view, the subject who experienced the past would no longer be around, and I would not have been around to experience the past.

Nor, this argument continues, would any of my anticipation of future states be genuine anticipation, since I could not expect to be around to enjoy them. So, since memory is necessarily of my past, and anticipation necessarily of my future, without a past and future that are *mine* there would be no memory or anticipation at all. But without memory and anticipation there could be no temporality—no sense of time—to any of my experience, and with no temporality there *is no* experience; there would be no time at which anything ever happened. Hence, my continued existence over time is a necessary condition of any experience at all.

Let us now assess this argument. It makes all the sense in the world to accept the premises of this transcendental argument: We do have experience, and our experience is temporal; that is, we experience our present as poised not between an *abstract* past and future, but as poised between *our* past and future. And we should grant the proponents of this argument the premises that we do have memories, and that memory requires not just that there was a past experience, but that that past experience was—at least in some sense—*mine,* and that in memory I represent myself as both the subject of that past experience and as the subject of the present memory. And the same goes for anticipation: I must anticipate *my* future, not some future in general.

The questions we must ask, though, are these: (1) Does the fact that I have had experiences in the past and (hopefully) will have them in the future require that I have a persistent *self?* (2) Does the fact that memory and anticipation *represent* me to myself as identical over time mean that I must *be* identical over time in order to remember the past and to anticipate the future? Or is it possible that a self-less person could be the subject of memory and anticipation, represented in those attitudes as identical over time despite there being no self that persists from past to future? To ask these questions is to question the entailment between the premises and the conclusion of this influential argument. And just as in the case of the arguments for synchronic identity, we will see that there is no such entailment. This argument, like those, turns out to be invalid, and so provides no reason to believe in a self.

Once again, thinking about corporate or institutional states and processes can help here. We speak easily about "institutional memory," where that memory is carried by a company, or a college, or even a family, without its being carried by any single member. Such memory may extend over many generations, passed from one individual to another, sometimes orally, sometimes in a written archive, sometimes as a set of practices that each generation learns from the preceding, or even as a pattern of charges on a silicon wafer.

But this hardly implies that each complex institution must have a persistent self to make its persistence through time and its institutional memory possible. To be sure, it is important for an institution, when it remembers an event in its past, to have been involved in that event, and institutional planning requires the assumption of the continued existence of that institution in the future. But that hardly entails that the institution has a *self*. After all, like Hume's church, an organization can persist through time, can retain records of its past, and can plan for the future without there being any single component or core to its being that persists, that retains its institutional memory, or that forges its plans.

The same can be true regarding our own temporal extension. Recall the important distinction we drew in the first chapter between the person and the self. The memory and anticipation argument is a good argument for the existence of the *person* in the past and the future. To remember having met you in Ulan Bator five years ago, I must be the same *person* who encountered you then, and to anticipate meeting you five years hence in Wagga Wagga, I must think of myself as the same *person* I am now five years hence (and *mutatis mutandis* for the way I think of your diachronic identity). But that kind of identity, like the kind of institutional identity presupposed by institutional memory and anticipation, does not presuppose the identity of a *self* that persists through all of the changes I suffer over that decade; it only presupposes psychophysical causal connectedness, that is, the identity and persistence of a *person*.

The fact that my mental state now counts as a memory reflects its causal history and its content: it was caused initially by our encounter in that yurt, and it has that meeting as its current content. No relation to a self is required to underwrite those connections. The fact that my anticipation of our meeting at the cricket ground in a few years' time is an anticipation has to do with its content, and my representation of my *personal* continuity over that stretch of time; again, no need for a self here.

So, the transcendental argument for the existence of the self on the grounds of the need to explain diachronic identity fails in the same way that the transcendental argument from synchronic identity fails. In each case, the only identity that follows from the premises—the only identity that is required to explain our experience—is *personal* identity, not the numerical identity of an enduring self.[14] Once again, even if we grant the premises of this argument, they constitute no reason to believe the conclusion.

We have now seen that these transcendental arguments—whether grounded in the supposed synchronic unity of the subject, in the synchronic unity of the object, or in the diachronic unity of the subject—fail to establish the reality of a transcendent self. At best, they deliver the reality of the *person*; at worst, they simply beg the question. In the next chapter, we consider arguments for the existence not of a transcendent, substantial self, but of a more minimal self. Some of these arguments will also be transcendental in form. Like those we have just canvassed, they each have both classical and contemporary instances.[15]

5

The Self Strikes Back II

THE MINIMAL SELF

Minimal Selves: Reflexivity Arguments

Many contemporary proponents of the reality of a self grant that the critiques of the transcendental arguments we addressed in the previous chapter are successful. They also grant that the conclusion those arguments aim to derive—the reality of a transcendent self—is too strong, too metaphysically rich for contemporary tastes. Instead, they argue for a more modest, stripped-down self. This self, they emphasize, it is not the original, primordial, substantial, transcendent self that is accepted in the orthodox Indian traditions or by Kant, the existence of which is defended in the arguments we have just discussed. It is, however, they insist, a real self.

There are two principal views in this neighborhood. The first is often called the doctrine of a "minimal self," or a bare subjectivity. We will see that that doctrine comes in two principal forms, one grounded in a commitment to the reflexivity of awareness, and one grounded in an account of the phenomenology of perception. The second is the doctrine of a "narrative self," a self that is constructed through our own autobiographical thought processes. Each has important contemporary partisans, and the arguments for each have classical antecedents. This chapter will explore the arguments for these positions. I will present the arguments in the words of their proponents as much as possible, both to be fair to them, and to give a sense of what the contemporary literature feels like. I will argue that we should not accept them.

I begin with the idea of a minimal self, a view advanced in slightly different ways by Galen Strawson, Evan Thompson, and Dan Zahavi.[1] The first arguments we will consider are those that rely on a thesis of the reflexivity of awareness. Strawson is explicit about the nature of this minimal self:

> I propose to take the unchallengeable, ontologically non-committal notion of the subject of experience in a minimal or 'thin' way. . . . I mean the subject considered specifically as something 'inner', something mental, the 'self', if you like, the inner 'locus' of consciousness considered just as such.[2]

I like this statement, because it confirms so beautifully the fact that even sophisticated contemporary philosophers take the core of our being to be our existence as selves, and that they take this to be "unchallengeable" and "ontologically non-committal." That is, Strawson thinks not only that this is obvious, but also that it does not commit to us to the existence of anything whose reality is controversial.

As we have already seen, despite the massive prejudice in favor of such a view, it is not only not *unchallengeable*, but it has been widely challenged; despite Strawson's claim that it is *ontologically noncommittal*, the view that we are selves is ontologically rich, and, if my arguments to this point are correct, it is also false. Indeed, in the very next sentence, Strawson belies his own characterization of this position as ontologically noncommittal when he commits himself explicitly to an "inner locus of consciousness." And happily, despite his claim that the reality of such a self is unchallengeable, Strawson rises to the challenge of proving its existence. He argues for the thesis that we are self-aware selves, a thesis he dubs *USA* (Universal Self-Awareness), emphasizing both the putative fact that we are selves, and that these selves are necessarily self-aware.[3]

We will turn to Strawson's argument shortly. But first let us be clear about the thesis he wishes to defend, and about the overall structure of his position. Keeping the big picture in view will help us not to get lost in the details of the argument (and there are a lot of details; one must read with care). At first glance, Strawson is simply arguing for the thesis of the *reflexivity of awareness*. That thesis is that every act of awareness is bipolar in structure, having two distinct objects. On the one hand, an act of awareness is directed on the manifest *object* of awareness. On the other hand, at the same time every such act is directed on the subjective state itself, or at least on the fact that one is aware. So, according to those who defend the reflexivity thesis, when I am aware of an apple on my desk, I am *ipso facto* aware of the fact that I am aware of that apple. Moreover, this awareness of my awareness is not conferred by a second cognitive state directed on the perception—what philosophers call a *higher-order cognition*—but is an aspect of the perceptual awareness of the apple itself.

This is taken by friends of reflexivity to be the case for any conscious state: we are, Strawson claims, never aware without being—in that very act of awareness—also aware of our own subjectivity. This is a controversial (and, I believe, a false) thesis.

But it is defended both in certain classical Indian schools and by many contemporary philosophers of mind who are influenced by the European phenomenological tradition.[4]

Strawson *is* defending the reflexivity thesis, but that is not the end of the story, and that is not why we are interested in his views. The reason for our interest is that Strawson defends the reflexivity of awareness in order to argue that this reflexivity is grounded in the reality of a self-aware self. This argument is hence—just as it was in classical India—one contemporary strategy for defending the reality of the self. Here is the argument for reflexivity in Strawson's own words:

> [P1] Awareness is (necessarily) a property of a subject of awareness.
> [P2] Awareness of a property of x is *ipso facto* awareness of x.
> [P1] and [P2] entail
> [3] Any awareness, A1, of any awareness, A2 entails awareness of the subject of A2.
> And we can get [2] = USA from [3] if we add
> [4] All awareness involves awareness of awareness
> or rather (the key premise):
> [5] All awareness involves awareness of itself.[5]

Let us see how this argument is meant to go, and just what is wrong with it. We will explore it in considerable detail, as it is such a clear and explicit argument for this thesis, and careful attention to it will shed light on the confusions at the heart of both the instinctive self illusion and the philosophical elaborations of that illusion. We will then turn to the use of reflexivity to defend the reality of the self.

Strawson claims parenthetically that [P1], the first premise—that awareness must be a property of a *subject of awareness*—is a necessary truth, one that cannot be doubted. But it not only is *not* a necessary truth; we will see that it is simply false. Moreover, it at least begs the question in this context. To say that awareness is necessarily a property of a subject of awareness, while perhaps seeming to be an innocent grammatical point, in fact commits the very fallacy of reification that we addressed in chapter 2. That is the fallacy of going from the mere fact of awareness to the existence of a *subject* of awareness.

To draw this inference is kind of like going from the claim that it is raining to the claim that there is something that is the agent of raining, that is *doing* the raining. To presume that the very fact of awareness entails the existence of a subject—in the strong sense that Strawson and other friends of the self have in mind—is to assume that which is to be proven, *viz.*, that awareness presupposes a self. The parallel to the failure of Descartes's *cogito* argument in which he goes from the mere fact of thinking to the existence of a substantial subject of thought is striking.

This argument is question-begging because, as we saw in the context of our discussion of Descartes's argument in chapter 2, awareness can be the result of the cooperation of a number of psychophysical processes, and it can consist in a number of relations between aspects of a person and aspects of their environment. Awareness is most plausibly an umbrella property that reflects an extremely complex set of underlying properties and relations. If this is the case, awareness can be present—a person can be aware—without there being any *single thing that is aware,* just as a nation or a corporation can act without there being any singular entity that performs that action.

Now, we might say that if there is awareness, *something* is aware, e.g., a person, just as we can say that when a corporation sells a product, something, e.g., the corporation, is the seller. But it is plain in that case that we do not thereby implicate a localizable single *thing* that is a subject or an agent, only a broad set of processes and events. So, even if we *grant* that awareness always has a subject-object structure, the defender of the reality of the self is not entitled to the premise that the subject is singular, and so cannot presume that it is a *self*.

But there is also a second, deeper problem with this argument. This first premise, as we have just noted, presupposes that awareness must have a subject-object structure. We granted that premise for the sake of argument, and we saw that even then we do not get a good argument for the reality of a self. But we can also question that presupposition. The idea that awareness always has a subject-object structure—with a subject characterized by a kind of interiority, as opposed to the exterior object that is somehow brought into awareness in that interior space— might well be an illusion of consciousness. That is, it might be a fabrication, not a basic reality. To put the point more precisely, the conviction that awareness is fundamentally a relation between an independent subject and a substantially distinct object may be the result of a cognitive illusion, just as the conviction that we are selves is not the consequence of looking inside and simply finding a self, but of cognitive illusion.

To be sure, this is how awareness appears to us when we introspect. But that is pretty weak evidence. Once again, when we see them, the two lines of the Müller-Lyer illusion appear to be of different lengths: appearance is no guarantee of reality. It makes a great deal of biological, psychological, and ecological sense instead to think of awareness as a constant modulation of the open interaction between an organism and its environment, of the adjustment of the state of the organism and attunement of the posture and goals of the organism as its senses and movements interact with the world it inhabits. In other words, we can think of awareness as a mode of embedding of the organism in its world, instead of as the relation between an interior subject and an exterior object, even if that is how it appears to us in introspection. To think of awareness in this way is to take seriously the idea that we don't stand against the world as subjects that detect its properties or agents that act on it, but instead are part of the world, and that awareness is more an attunement to our environment than a recording in our minds of what is going on outside. This approach to cognition, which is called the "embedded, embodied, enactive" model of cognition, is gaining wide acceptance among philosophers and cognitive scientists.[6]

The view that introspection may be wildly deceptive, called "illusionism," is also gaining increasing currency in the philosophy of mind today, inspired in part by the analysis of human existence developed by twentieth- and twenty-first-century existential phenomenologists.[7] But it is very old in India, and underlies the idea of the nonduality of consciousness articulated both in the Vedānta school and in Buddhism. Philosophers in each of these traditions argued that we are subject to pervasive confusion not only regarding the external world, but also regarding our own nature and regarding the structure of our experience. So, we should treat Strawson's first premise with suspicion. This suspicion, we have seen, is justified for two reasons: first, our existence may well be that of a complex set of subjective processes as opposed to that of a single self; second, the subject-object structure of awareness that he takes for granted may well be illusory.

So much for the first premise: it is at least problematic. The second premise, [P2]—that awareness of a property of x is *ipso facto* awareness of x—is clearly false. I might well be aware of a flash of red in the periphery of my visual field but not be aware of the cardinal that flew by. I might have a sense that I am being followed, without any awareness of the spy who stalks me.[8] So, while the first two premises *do* entail the third statement in the argument, that argument rests on shaky premises, the first of which we have seen to be quite possibly false, and the second of which is definitely false.

Step [3]—the claim that any awareness of another awareness entails awareness of the subject of that awareness itself—is the conclusion of the argument. But Strawson points out that we only get from [P2] to this conclusion via steps [4] and [5] (which is really a restatement of [4], as he also points out). So, let us consider those steps, the latter of which Strawson calls "the key premise." It should be clear that they are each also false. [4] says that when I am aware of an apple on my desk, I must also be aware that I am aware of an apple on my desk, and not through a distinct thought, a higher-order awareness, but in that very act of awareness itself. [5]—the claim that all awareness involves awareness of awareness—makes that fact explicit, and so is really a clarification of [4], not an additional step in the argument.

Now, as I noted above, [5], which is the classic thesis of the reflexivity of awareness, is not without heavyweight defenders. Aristotle and the Indian Buddhist philosopher Dharmakīrti each use a regress argument to defend this thesis. Abstracting from the different details of their respective presentations, it goes like this:

[i] Suppose that I am aware of an object O in virtue of being in a psychological state P (perhaps a perceptual state, or a memory state, or an idle daydream about O). For instance, I might be aware of my dog Talisker because I see him, or remember a walk we took together. Let's suppose it is because I now see him.

[ii] I am either aware of P or I am not. (That is, in this case, I am either aware of seeing Talisker or I am not.)

[iii] If I am not aware of P, then I am not aware of O. (If I am not aware of seeing him, then I am not aware of Talisker himself.)

[iv] So, I must be aware of P. (So, I must be aware of seeing him.)

[v] The state P′ in virtue of which I am aware of P must be P itself *or* a higher-order state P″. (The state that makes me aware that I am seeing him must be that same state or a higher-order state of awareness of that seeing.)

[vi] If it is a higher-order state, it must also be conscious, and so requires a further higher-order state P‴ in order to be conscious.

[vii] This entails that if, in order for any state to be conscious, a higher-order state is required, any conscious state requires an infinite hierarchy of higher-order states, which is absurd.

[viii] *So*, if P discloses O, P itself must disclose P. (SO, if my seeing Talisker discloses his presence, it must disclose that state of seeing him as well.)

There are at least two things wrong with this argument. First, as we have seen, premise [iii] of the present argument for reflexivity, which is a version of Strawson's conclusion, is almost certainly false. I can be aware of what is going on around me without being simultaneously aware of that awareness. Now, one might think that [iii] would follow from the fact that awareness is always a relation between a subject and the object of which that subject is aware. But it doesn't. We often stand in relations to something else without standing in that same relation to ourselves. So, just as I can stand beside you without standing beside myself, I can be aware of you without being aware of myself.

Here is another way to see that premise [iii] must be false. It *must* be possible to be aware of an object without being aware of how we know that object. When you see a tree, for instance, you do so by using your eyes. Nonetheless, even though your eyes are among the instruments that mediate your awareness, they are not present in the awareness: to be aware of the tree is not to be aware of your eyes. Moreover, your eyes are not the only instruments that mediate that awareness. There are a host of neural and cognitive structures that enable you to see the tree, such as your optic nerve, and edge-detection algorithms computed in your visual system. You aren't aware of *these*, either. But these organs and processes are the very components of your subjectivity, the things that present the tree to you. To say that you are not aware of them is therefore to say that you are not aware of the awareness. So, the reflexivity thesis is at least uncertain, definitely implausible, and probably simply false. Since it is an essential step in this argument for the existence of the self, that argument is in trouble.

But things get worse: even if we were to grant [iii], the crucial regress argument for reflexivity fails to establish it. It confuses what would be a vicious regress of *actual* states of awareness with a benign regress of *possible* states of awareness. Here is the point: we might grant a *true* version of [iii]:

[iii*] It is always *possible* to *become* aware of any state of awareness through a higher-order state.

So, we might say plausibly, if I am aware of Talisker, it is possible for me to become aware of that awareness. I could do so just by reflecting on my current state of mind, something that we all *sometimes* do. That awareness involves a thought distinct from the original perception of the dog—a second-order state directed on and disclosing the first-order perceptual state that discloses him. And it might then be possible for me to consider that second-order state in a third-order awareness, and so on. That seems like a pretty good general account of introspection.

But that regress is harmless. To claim that it is vicious is akin to mounting the following argument against my being able to count to 2: if I count to 2, I can always count to 3, and then to 4 . . . . So, being able to count to 2 entails being able to count to every natural number, which requires the ability to perform an infinite number of arithmetic tasks. So, I cannot count to 2. That, of course, is a terrible argument. If counting to 2 required me actually to count through all of the natural numbers, it would be impossible to do so. But this argument only shows that I *can* always go on, even if I choose not to do so. It might deliver the fact that the natural numbers are infinite, but not that counting to any natural number is an infinite task.

That is why this counting regress is harmless. And the regress argument against the possibility of counting has the same structure as the regress argument against the claim that self-knowledge is achieved through higher-order awareness. That argument can only show that any higher-order awareness *could* become the object of a further higher-order awareness, not that it *does* (unless one presupposes the claim that any awareness presupposes actual awareness of that awareness—but, that, once again, is the conclusion to be proven, and can't be used as a premise in the argument). It follows that Strawson's claim that all awareness is reflexive fails, and with it the argument that all awareness discloses a self, leaving the claim that there is a self undefended.[9]

I think that this conclusion—that all awareness involves an awareness of my *self*—is implausible on its face. When I introspect and notice that I am experiencing a headache, or seeing a sunset, this may deliver awareness of the headache or of my perceptual state. But it is a real stretch to say that it also delivers awareness of a subject standing behind those states. And, if I am truly immersed in that experience, my own subjectivity is the furthest thing from my mind. (We will return to this point in chapter 6.) If I am just a stream of psychophysical processes, there may be nothing beyond that stream of which to be aware; that is the view that I have been defending. To simply presume that there is something that lies behind it is, once again, to assume the conclusion that Strawson is trying to establish.

This has been a long train of reasoning. So, let us now sum up what is wrong with Strawson's attempt to rehabilitate the self. His argument, like those we considered in the previous chapter, is transcendental in form. It presumes that the framework of subject-object duality is an accurate representation of the basic structure of experience, and then asks what we must be like in order for experience to be necessarily so structured.

In this case, we see that the premise—the *explanandum*—is to be rejected. It is one thing to say that we habitually thematize our experience through the framework of subject-object duality, at least when we are introspective, and another to say that we simply find that duality in experience itself. The only legitimate *explanandum* is our *commitment* to the subject-object framework, not the framework itself, and that commitment can be explained as a cognitive illusion, taking a feature of our experience that our mind constructs and superimposes for one that we just discover. There is therefore no argument here for the reflexivity of awareness, and so no argument on that basis for the reality of the self.

To accept Strawson's argument would be like noticing that we see the two lines of the Müller-Lyer illusion to be of different lengths and then trying to figure out how the arrowheads lengthened one and shortened the other. A better option would be to ask what it is about our perceptual system that leads us to see them that way *despite the fact that we know that they are of equal length.* This takes us back to the sense in which the self, and the subject-object duality with which it is imbricated, are *illusions.* They are the way we take ourselves and our experience to be, not the way that we, or our experience, actually exist; to take what is illusory to exist in the way it appears is like assuming that there must be some depth to the water in a mirage, and that it can quench our thirst.

This is not the only kind of argument from reflexivity for the existence of the self to gain traction in recent discussions. Evan Thompson[10] develops a different argument from reflexivity for the existence of the self, an argument with roots in classical India, due originally to the Buddhist philosopher Dignāga. This argument, although similar to Strawson's in its commitment to reflexivity, understands reflexivity differently—not as the explicit awareness of one's own subjectivity, but as a merely implicit sense of ownership of one's own experiences. Despite this difference in detail, the arguments are very similar in form, and our reply will be very similar.

Dignāga argues not for the existence of the self (after all, he was a Buddhist and so committed to the doctrine of no-self), but simply for the reflexivity of awareness. Nonetheless, just as Strawson uses reflexivity as an argument for the self, Thompson updates Dignāga's version of that argument into an argument for the reality of the self. The argument has two connected parts, the first of which is the Buddhist argument for the reflexivity of awareness mobilized by Dignāga, and the second of

which is the direct argument that this reflexivity entails the reality of a self.[11]

Here is part 1: When I remember last night's sunset, I remember *my seeing* last night's sunset. That is one memory, not
two. And the memory is the retrieval of that experience. Since
it is one memory, the proponent of reflexivity argues, there was
one experience. So, the experience of the sunset and the experience of *my seeing* the sunset must be the same. Therefore, every
experience is also an experience of my having that experience.

If part 1 is successful (and I will argue shortly that it is not), it
gets us to the conclusion that all perceptual experience is also
experience of experience, and that is the reflexivity thesis. To get
from there to the self, Thompson adds the following steps: The
only way that I can remember last night's sunset (as opposed to
fantasizing about it) is to be the same subject now as the subject
who experienced the sunset, and, in virtue of that fact, the same
subject who experienced *my* experience of that sunset. That is,
the *I* who experienced the experience of the sunset and the *I*
who now experiences the memory must be the same *I*. I could
not, for instance, remember *your* experience of that sunset. Thus,
the *I* that is the subject must endure through time, and must be
a self. This is part 2.

Unfortunately for the defender of the self, each of these two
sub-arguments is fallacious. Part 1 relies on a radical misunderstanding of how memory works, a misunderstanding that was
even evident to many medieval Indian and Tibetan philosophers.
That misunderstanding involves taking memory to be a straightforward retrieval in the mind of a past experience, like a reactiva-
tion of the past perception, or the recovery of a photocopy of that
experience. But that is not how memory works; it is not the *representation* of a preserved experience stored and then reexam-
ined when called to mind. Instead, it is a *reconstruction* of the past,

or, in other words, a cognitive fabrication. Successful memory is not the careful preservation of an image, newsreel, or text in the mind, but rather a successful reconstruction of a past event. Errors in memory are not degradations in a photograph kept on file; they are instead the construction of an account of the past that is at odds with what actually happened.[12]

This does not mean that memory is just imagination. There is a difference, but this difference concerns only the distinct causal ancestries of a present cognitive state. Perceptual experience is more salient as a cause of memory than of imagination. But this is a difference of degree, not of kind; to be a memory is only to be the effect of a particular kind of causal chain originating in an experience. The intermediate steps in that chain include a host of brain and cognitive processes of which we are largely unaware, and which are each responsible for any memory we construct, even though that construction may feel like the retrieval of an intact perceptual snapshot.

All memory is thus somewhat imaginative; all imagination relies on memory. So, even when I do actually construct a memory that thematizes my own subjectivity, that is no argument for the claim that that subjectivity was thematized in the original experience, and so no argument for reflexivity.[13] So, once again, even if we adopt this thinner notion of reflexive awareness advocated by Thompson, there is no reason to think that all awareness is reflexive, and so this argument for the existence of the self fails as well.

But even if we were to grant the reflexivity of experience for the sake of argument, this would not get us anywhere near an argument for the existence of the self. This is because the second part of the argument is equally fallacious (as Buddhist proponents of reflexivity in classical India also pointed out). For once again, if we see memory as the outcome of a sequence of cognitive processes, even if we grant that one can only remember one's own experiences, everything hinges on *what one is.*

Everyone in this debate will grant that to remember last night's sunset now, I must be the same *person* who saw that sunset last night. But that does not entail that I am a *self.* As we have seen, that would require that some single thing persists as the *basis* of that psychophysical continuum from last night to tonight—some underlying *substance.*

Nothing in the argument is even relevant to that supposition, though. All that the second part of the argument gets me is the continuity of a sequence of cognitive events starting with the perception of the sunset and ending with my memory of it. That is no different in principle from the sequences involved in institutional memory we discussed in chapter 4. So that kind of continuity is consistent with my being a selfless person. The memory argument hence would also fail to establish the existence of a self even if we granted the reflexivity claim.[14]

Let's briefly take stock of where we are in this discussion. We are addressing contemporary arguments (albeit with classical antecedents) for the existence of a minimal self, a self that is meant to be less robust than a substantial self, but nonetheless, a unified, continuing subject of experience, an agent of action, distinct from mind and body. We have examined two versions of arguments for such a self that depend on the idea of the reflexivity of awareness and we have found them wanting. We will now turn to three examples of a second approach to arguing for the existence of a minimal self, each of which originates in the European phenomenological tradition, in order of an increasingly minimal conception of that self and its basis. The first of these depends on the idea that all of our experience has a special property of *for-me-ness.* The second depends upon the idea that there is a special kind of intransitive or immediate self-consciousness that discloses the self to us. The third appeals to pre-reflective self-awareness. We will consider and reject each of these. Finally, we will address a fourth, somewhat different approach to defending a minimal self: the idea that the self is a narrative construction.

Minimal Selves: *For-me-ness*

Dan Zahavi presents an argument for the existence of the self that is grounded on what he calls the *for-me-ness* or *mine-ness* of experience. It is instructive that he uses this terminology, as it emphasizes that he is in fact defending the very target of the Buddhist arguments against a self that we examined in chapter 2. Buddhist philosophers in India and Tibet often characterize the view that there is a self as the *twofold self-grasping,* or the *grasping onto I and being-mine.* The second term in this phrase expresses the idea that the objects of experience or the components of the person must be understood in relation to an independent subject, that they must be *owned* by subjectivity. That subjectivity is the self.[15] Here is how Zahavi puts it:

> If we compare [the perception of] a green apple with [the recollection of] a yellow lemon, there has been a change of both the object and the intentional type. Does such a change leave nothing unchanged in the experiential flow? Is the difference between the first experience and the last experience as radical as the difference between my current experience and the current experience of someone else? We should deny this. Whatever their type, whatever their object, there is something that the different experiences have in common. Not only is the first experience retained by the last experience, but the different experiences are all characterized by

the same fundamental first-person character. They are all characterized by what we might call a dimension of *for-me-ness* or *mineness*.[16]

Zahavi argues here that whatever distinguishes our various experiences on the *object* side (eggs vs. apples; whiteness vs. redness), our own experiences have something in common on the *subject* side that the experiences of others all lack, namely *for-me-ness* or *mineness*. This is a crucial step in his larger argument: since this *for-me-ness* is a direct relation to a (minimal) self, there must, he argues, be such a minimal self. Zahavi characterizes this elusive property as follows:

> The for-me-ness or mineness in question is not a quality like scarlet, sour, or soft. It doesn't refer to a specific experiential content, to a specific *what*.... Rather, it refers to the distinct givenness or *how* of experience. It refers to the first-personal presence of experience.... [A]nybody who denies the for-me-ness or mine-ness of experience simply fails to recognize an essential constitutive aspect of experience. Such a denial would be tantamount to a denial of the first-person perspective. It would entail the view that my own mind is either not given to me at all—I would be mind-blind or self-blind—or present to me in exactly the same way as the minds of others.[17]

Just as we saw Strawson presuming that the existence of the self is "unchallengeable," here we see Zahavi asserting that to deny the reality of this *for-me-ness* "simply fails to recognize an essential constitutive aspect of experience." It is always a good idea to be suspicious of this kind of table-pounding. Just as I think that we *should* challenge the existence of the self, I think that we should wonder whether *for-me-ness* is an essential element of our experience, and, even if we thought that it was, whether this would entail that there is a *me* for whom my experience is present, where that *me* is understood as a *self*. We will now see that there is reason to reject both of these claims.

First, note that Zahavi argues that the property of *for-me-ness* is what distinguishes my own experiences from those of others. But that can't be. For, if he is even close to correct, *your* experiences have this property as well; from *your* perspective those experiences are *for me*, just as from my perspective, *my* experiences are *for me*. If all experiences have this property *essentially*, then we can't use it to distinguish among them. Moreover, if this is really the property that distinguishes my own experiences from yours—the property that lets me know that they are mine, and not yours—I should be able to compare my experiences with yours, find *for-me-ness* in mine, but not in yours, and so come to know that mine are mine and that yours are yours. And that makes no sense whatsoever.

This part of the argument is hence just a shell game. It might well *appear* that the only way that I could know when I have an experience that it is mine and not yours would be to detect some telltale property of that experience that reveals it to be mine. In that case, if it lacked that property, then on noticing the experience, I would recognize it as *yours*, not *mine*. But I can't first have an experience and then wonder whose it is. Simply to have an experience is for it to be mine. So, there is no property of all of my experiences the presence of which announces them as mine, simply because there is no property without which I would know them to be someone else's.

What would it be like to have an experience, notice that there was no *for-me-ness* in it, and then conclude that it was yours? This is one way of making the broader point that experiences themselves don't have their own subjective properties; the properties of experiences are all properties of the *contents* of experience, not of the *subject*.[18] The fact that my experiences are mine can never entail that I am a *self*, as opposed to a *person*, just as the fact that my dog is mine can't entail that I am a self, as opposed to a person.

There is a reason that Zahavi's argument has a ring of plausibility: it trades on the correct observation that you have *your* experiences and I have *mine*. But that banal fact doesn't imply that mine are mine in virtue of possessing some mysterious property. After all, the fact that I refer to myself as "I" and refer to you as "you" doesn't mean that I have *I-ness* and you have *you-ness*. Since the fact that I am me and you are you doesn't implicate any special *I-ness* and *you-ness* properties, I don't need to detect them in order to tell myself from you. In exactly the same sense, the fact that my experiences are mine and yours are yours doesn't entail that I detect *for-me-ness* in mine and not in yours, even though I know when I have them that my experiences are indeed mine.

Not only can this putative property not do the work of distinguishing between streams of experience, but we should wonder whether it is in fact "an essential and constitutive aspect of experience" at all. As I have now argued several times, while it might be true that we sometimes thematize ourselves as subjects in our higher-order awareness of our mental states, it is almost certainly not true that we *always* do so. When we are immersed in activity, we are aware of the world around us, aware of the foci of our attention, but often not at all aware of ourselves as subjects. And if that is right, then we do not experience *for-me-ness* whenever we experience anything else.

Moreover, as we noted above, subject-object duality is better understood as a superimposition on a basically nondual experience than as an essential or a constitutive aspect of that experience. Subject-object duality, that is, reflects the way we represent our experience to ourselves (when we are actively doing so), not the way we actually experience the world, just as the apparent difference between the lengths of the lines in the Müller-Lyer illusion is a feature of our perception of the lines, not of the lines themselves. Even that superimposition requires a nondual immersion in introspection! So, Zahavi's argument—one representative of the approach of many (but not all) of the "new phenomenologists" who defend the reality of the self—fails at three points: it fails to identify a property that distinguishes experiences as *mine*; it fails to demonstrate that that property is essential to experience; and it fails to demonstrate that even were that property detected in all experiences, that it would reveal the existence of a self.

There is yet one more problem with this argument, and it connects directly to our previous discussion of subject-object duality as illusory. This philosophical exercise begins with the intuition that experience involves a kind of interiority, an inner space in which experience occurs. The *for-me-ness* to which Zahavi and others refer is a way of indicating location in this interior space. But this inner space is a myth, or, at best, a metaphor for an illusion. It is not the cranium, or any other location in the interior of our bodies. In fact, there is nothing to which we can point of which our subjectivity is the interior. Experience, as I have been arguing, is better understood as a complex *set of relations* between a complex person (or another kind of organism) and the other complex aspects of the environment it inhabits, not as a replication of that environment in a dark inner space in consciousness. This is a context in which the most natural metaphor only gets us into trouble when we try to spell it out.[19]

Indian Buddhist philosophers talk about the tendency to see experience in terms of this replication of the world of objects in an interior space as an instance of *ahaṃkāra*, literally, *the construction of an I.* The emphasis here is on *construction.* We start with the metaphor of the inner and outer as a way of distinguishing ourselves from the rest of the world. This metaphor makes a certain amount of sense as a way of gesturing towards the greater access we have to our own psychological and somatic states than we do to those of other objects and persons. We then reify it, forgetting that it was only a metaphor in the first place, and freezing the metaphorical subjective side into an entity, or an inner space in which special inner events occur, hence creating a self as the referent of *I.*

And we can go further. Even if we *granted* that the self so created was *real,* the very best we could get out of an argument such as Zahavi's would be not the self we reify and with which we identity—not the object of negation of no-self arguments— but instead a succession of momentary selves, one for each moment of experience.[20] Nothing in Zahavi's argument yields the endurance of the subjective side of experience, only—even *were it successful*—a subjective side of *each* experience. This is not the controller, the center of consciousness, the agent, the owner of mind and body that we take ourselves to be when we think of ourselves as selves. At best, this is the elephant, not the snake. The argument in effect concedes that there is no snake in the wall in the first place.[21]

Minimal Selves: An Argument from Intransitive Self-Consciousness

So much for arguments from *for-me-ness.* Let us now turn to the second major line of argument advanced by the new phenomenologists: Evan Thompson's argument for a special kind of intransitive self-consciousness that is meant to deliver the reality of a minimal self.[22] This argument is closely connected to those we have just discussed, but Thompson's approach attempts to evade the problems besetting a reflexivity theory by treating self-consciousness not as reflexive, but as intransitive.

A transitive consciousness is one in which a subject is aware of something else, as when I am aware of the apple on my desk. To be transitively aware of oneself would be to take oneself as an *object*, as when one looks into a mirror. The reflexive awareness we discussed above, is, despite its reflexivity, transitive in this sense. This is *not* what Thompson has in mind when he appeals to intransitive self-awareness in order to show that the self is disclosed in consciousness. Instead, he wants to argue that awareness makes us directly aware of our subjectivity, not as an object, but as an immediately experienced aspect of our awareness of any object. Here is how he puts it:

> [Every] intentional experience both presents (or re-represents) its intentional object and discloses itself, but this disclosure is intransitive. . . . Although the "what-question" can arise for the transitive component of an intentional experience, it cannot arise for the intransitive component of pre-reflective self-awareness. In sum . . . every transitive consciousness of an object is pre-reflectively and intransitively self-conscious.[23]

I can always ask *what* I see, hear, feel, or remember. That is the *what* question. Thompson emphasizes that this kind of question always makes sense with respect to an object of experience. But, he argues, this kind of question does not make sense for the subject. I cannot ask *what* sees the apple I now see. Thus, he concludes, that subject must be taken for granted as existing, albeit in a minimal way, not as substance, but as that self which is disclosed in this intransitive self-consciousness.

Should we be convinced? I think not. The clear kinship of this argument to that proffered by Zahavi suggests that it suffers from the same kinds of difficulties, and this is in fact the case. Our work in the previous section allows us to state the difficulties briefly. First, we *can* ask *what* is disclosed in a non-transitive way. We can grant that when I see an apple, the fact that I am seeing an apple is disclosed. Nonetheless, it does *not* follow that a *self* is disclosed as the subject of that seeing, only *that an apple is seen*. Nothing follows regarding what is doing that seeing. If what is at stake is the difference between a self and a person, nothing at all follows from the fact that I see an object that could settle that question.[24]

Second, as I argued above, the fact that a subject-object duality appears in my own introspective awareness of the experience of seeing the apple does not even mean that there is a subject to be disclosed, when that subject is understood as something standing over and against the object. It entails only that there is a perceptual process in which an embodied person is embedded, and that I introspectively represent that process as dual. Once again, so long as we do not confuse the person with the self, there is not even the appearance of an argument for the reality of a self to be found here, or even for the subject-object duality that entails the reality of a unitary subject. The argument from non-transitive self-consciousness thus fails as well to establish the reality of the self.

So far in this chapter we have gone from reflexive arguments, to arguments from a vague sense of *for-me-ness*, to arguments from intransitive self-awareness for the reality of a substantial self, each relying on a thinner reed in order to save the self. We have seen that despite their historical importance and current popularity, none are convincing. But that is not the end of the story. Perhaps that self-awareness is not reflexive, not directed on *for-me-ness*, and not even simply intransitive, but a kind of pre-reflective background to consciousness that nonetheless is sufficient to deliver the reality of the self. We will consider this last desperate strategy before turning to narrative accounts.

Pre-reflective Self-Awareness

Evan Thompson in his later work defends an even more minimal view of the self than that in his earlier work, one according to which the self is simply constituted by a kind of pre-reflective self-awareness, and it is worth quoting him on this issue. Responding to Thomas Metzinger's argument against the existence of a substantial, persistent self,[25] Thompson writes:

> The problem with this argument is that it rests on a tendentious concept of the self. Metzinger assumes that "self" means a personal essence inhering in an individual substance. He denies that there is such a thing and therefore concludes that selves do not exist. But this conclusion follows only given this concept of the self. His argument requires the premise that for something to be a self, it must be a single, unique, unified, and independent thing with a personal essence. Some philosophers have conceived of the self in this way, but many others have not.[26]

Note that the analysis of the self with which Thompson charges Metzinger is pretty much the one we have taken as our target so far. And Metzinger's choice to characterize the self in this way is not arbitrary. As we saw in the first chapter, this is the way that we instinctively take ourselves to exist. One might use the word *self* to refer to something else, and then demonstrate that that *other thing* exists. But to do that, as we will see that Thompson does, is to commit the error that Candrakīrti lampoons: dispelling a belief in an elephant to reassure oneself that there is no snake. Here is how Thompson suggests that we think of the self:

> Self-awareness takes different forms. According to phenom- enologists, a minimal form of self-awareness is a constant structural feature of any conscious experience. They call this kind of self-awareness "prereflective." This means that the awareness happens before we do any reflecting on our expe- rience and that it's implicit rather than explicit. The idea is that every conscious experience appears to itself, without any reflection or thought, as a conscious experience, or to put it another way, that all experiencing involves implicitly experiencing that very experiencing. . . . According to phe- nomenologists, prereflective self-awareness is necessary for the other kinds of self-awareness, and it constitutes the sense of self in its minimal form.[27]

Note that Thompson draws our attention to two matters that must be disentangled for clarity. The first is the *self*; the second is *self-awareness*. And it is the reality—and indeed the ubiquity—of implicit pre-reflective self-awareness on which Thompson insists here. This, we will see, is a species of the reflexive awareness we discussed earlier. But for now, let us see that one cannot argue from the reality—or even the necessity—of self-*awareness* to the reality of the *self*. I will begin by demonstrating the invalidity of the central inference in the argument. That is, I will show that it is quite possible to accept this implicit self-awareness as a real psychological phenomenon while taking the self to be nonexis- tent. In fact, that it is just what it is to say that the self is an illusion: that it appears to exist, but in fact does not.

Consider, as an analogy, the structure of our visual field. We experience it (pre-reflectively, implicitly, and ubiquitously) as uniformly colored, with no holes in it. But it is well known that this is an illusion, one we are wired to project. There is a hole at the very center of the visual field—a blind spot—where the optic nerve enters the retina, and so where there are no photoreceptive cells. Moreover, we are sensitive to color only in the middle of our visual field. Over half of that field is in fact available to the retina only in black and white. Our visual system fills in the hole and paints in the colors for us, despite receiving no information at all from the very center of the field, and no color information from the periphery. Our visual experience does not reflect what our senses deliver; it is a construction, not a registration.

Nonetheless, we remain blissfully unaware of this operation as we behold the visible world. One cannot, then, argue from the *awareness* of uniformity to the *actual* uniformity of that of which we are aware. And for the same reason, one cannot argue that simply because I am *self-aware,* there is a *self of which I am aware.* Note further that if this argument were sound, one could argue that because I have an awareness of being followed while walking down a lonely road in the dark, there is someone following me of whom I am aware.

We will return to this issue in a moment, as it is a serious problem at this stage of Thompson's argument. But first, let us ask whether the principal premise in the argument—the claim that "a minimal form of self-awareness is a constant structural feature of any conscious experience"—is true. I for one do not see why anyone would accept this claim. But in order to refute the claim, we must be clear about what Thompson has in mind. As he notes a bit later, this is not meant to be the claim that we are *explicitly* aware of ourselves in every moment, a claim that would be manifestly false.[28] We therefore cannot reply to Thompson by denying the reality of that explicit kind of self-awareness, as he will respond that we are confusing explicit with implicit awareness, and that correctly denying that we are *explicitly* self-aware whenever we are conscious does not undermine the claim that we are *implicitly* self-aware whenever we are conscious. So, let us ask what this minimal or implicit self-awareness that is less than explicit, reflective, self-awareness might be, and how it is meant to differ from having no self-awareness at all.

You are now reading the words on this page. You are aware of the words, and of the topic under discussion. Are you, in that act of reading and of thinking, also aware—even implicitly—of yourself being aware? Even when we bear in mind the claim that this is not meant to be explicit awareness, available in introspection, or the content of an occurrent thought, I see no reason to believe that I am. If that awareness were really a precondition of any other kind of awareness, it would appear to follow both that I could not be aware of the words without being aware of myself reading them *and* that I could not be aware of myself reading them unless I was also pre-reflectively aware of myself being pre-reflectively aware of being myself reading them.

A nasty regress looms. It is worth noting that this is a regress of *actual*, not *potential* awareness, and referring to it as *implicit, pre-thetic,* or *intransitive* does not make it any less *actual*. Each act of awareness, on this view, presupposes another actual pre-thetic awareness that makes it aware. And it is the fact that this is a regress of *actual* awarenesses, not merely potential awarenesses, that makes it vicious. To disarm the regress, a defender of this argument would have to take the awareness in question to be merely potential, and to rephrase the premise as the claim that I can always become aware of myself as subject whenever I am aware of something else, should I care to reflect.

The ensuing regress would then be harmless, like the counting regress we considered earlier. But this is cold comfort for the friend of reflexivity, for it replaces actual, immediate self-awareness with merely potential higher-order awareness of a cognitive state. So, the basic premise of this argument is at the very least problematic, and probably false. And a merely potential higher-order awareness is insufficient, as we have seen, to ground the reality of the self. It is merely the possibility that one cognitive state can take another as its object. Anyone who wants to use this argument to defend the existence of even a minimal self needs that awareness to be *actual,* and that lands one in the vicious regress.

So much for the premise of Thompson's argument. But suppose that we grant it, accepting for the sake of argument that I *am* pre-reflectively aware of myself in every moment of consciousness. The existence of a self would still not follow. To move from the relatively innocuous (although possibly psychologically false) claim that we have a *sense* that we are a self at each moment of our lives to the stronger claim that this is evidence that we have a self in the sense that we take ourselves to have one is a straightforward *non sequitur.* That inference requires a further premise, *viz.,* that this sense of self is veridical—that merely the fact that we have that cognitive state makes the belief to which it gives rise true.

That is a premise that neither Thompson nor any of the partisans of this position defends, and for good reason: to assume that premise in this context is to beg the question, since the very accuracy of our own sense of who we are is what is up for debate. One might attempt to avoid begging the question by retreating to the claim that the self just consists in the reflexive awareness of a moment of consciousness by itself, as Thompson suggests in the passage we just quoted. But as a defense of the existence of the self this is a nonstarter. Nobody takes themselves to be a moment of reflexive awareness in a moment of consciousness. That is Candrakīrti's elephant. To get to something that looks more like a self in this context, we would need to posit something standing behind *all* moments of consciousness that is aware of them. *That* would indeed be the serpent in the wall. But, as Thompson himself acknowledges, even a pervasive minimal implicit self-consciousness can't get you there. Thompson concludes:

> From the phenomenological perspective, the self is a multifaceted construction, made out of different kinds of self-awareness, not an unconstructed personal essence or independent thing. Given this viewpoint, there are no grounds for saying that the self is an illusion. . . . Although illusions are mental constructions, not all mental constructions are illusions. . . .
>
> There's a traditional Buddhist way to make this point. It requires making a terminological and conceptual distinction between "self" (*ātman*) and "person" (*pudgala*). If we restrict "self" to mean a personal essence that is the independent owner of experience and agent of action, and we use "person" to refer to the multifaceted construction that includes modes of self-awareness, then we can say that whereas the self is an illusion or nonexistent fiction, the person exists. In other words, from the perspective of Buddhist philosophy, my argument that the self is a construction can be taken as an argument for the claim that the person is a construction.[29]

This all sounds very plausible, but it takes us back to where we started. Thompson, like the man with the snake in the wall of his house, has redefined *self* to mean *person,* and has argued that the person is a real construction. He has then concluded that the self so understood is real. There is nothing wrong with redefining terms, and there is nothing wrong with using the world *self* to mean *person*. But nobody has ever denied that persons exist, or even that personhood is constructed. So, to argue that persons exist is beside the point. Thompson has therefore not successfully defended the reality of the self we instinctively posit. At best, he has only changed the meaning of the words, and conceded that we are persons, not selves.

This concludes our discussion of phenomenological approaches to defending the reality of a minimal self. Even the thinnest of these conceptions fails to capture a real self. We now turn to the final, most minimal contemporary strategy for rescuing the self—the idea that the self is a narrative construction. We will see, not surprisingly, that in thinning the self even further in order to save it, this strategy, too, ends up defending the reality of persons, and conceding the unreality of selves.

Persons and Narrative

Some proponents of the reality of the self would agree that none of the arguments we have just considered are any good. They concede that it makes no sense to talk of a substantial self, however minimal; despite their commitment to the reality of a self, they do not conceive of that self as a substance, or even in any sense as a primordial, independent self. Instead, these contemporary self-theorists argue, we each have a *constructed* or *narrative* self. Daniel Hutto defends the view that our identity is constituted by the autobiographical narratives we tell, and that these narratives are the basis of our subjectivity.[30] There is both something deeply right and something deeply wrong about this idea. Let us tease out the insight from the error. Here is what is right: our identities as persons in part consist in the roles we play in the collective narrative in which we figure. We have seen this idea introduced in chapter 3, and we will return to it in more detail in chapters 8 and 9. As persons, we play roles, and roles require a narrative context in order to make sense.

But we must be careful not to confuse the personhood constituted by these narratives with the kind of basic identity or pure subjectivity assigned to selves. It is one thing to say that our personhood is constituted by narrative, and another to say that our very subjectivity is. To be sure, persons are in part constituted through narratives, and through participation in the norm-governed practices that make narrative possible. Nonetheless, no proponent of the reality of the self—as distinct from the person—could take narrative as the basis of that reality. For the self is meant to be that which makes subjectivity possible in the first place, and we must already have subjectivity in place in order to be able to tell stories about ourselves.[31]

It follows that narrative identity cannot be the ultimate basis of subjectivity, even though it might well be the basis of personhood. Obviously, a proponent of the no-self view owes us an account of the basis of subjectivity, and we will come to that. But that is not the point here. The point is rather that a proponent of the reality of the self cannot appeal to narrative as its basis. To do so would be to abandon the project for which the self was posited in the first place and to confuse the self with the person.[32]

And this is why the distinction between the self and the person is so important. While persons are what we *are*, selves are what we *take ourselves to be*. And to take ourselves to be selves is to succumb to a pernicious and incoherent delusion, albeit a delusion that comes perfectly naturally to us. But to claim that because we are not selves, we are not persons, would be an equally egregious error, and that would amount to denying our own reality.

So, in order to affirm the reality of persons and to deny that of selves, we must be clear about the distinction between the two. We can agree with proponents of a narrative identity that the person is a construction and nonetheless that it is real, while denying that anything corresponds to the idea of the self. When we affirm the reality of the person while denying the reality of the self, we are not simply regimenting our use of words in some technical or artificial way; we are making space for the clarification of the nature of persons and for the dissolution of the fantasy of the self, each of which is important to understanding who and what we are.

I would add—following Candrakīrti, Locke, Hume, and others—that to understand the construction of personhood we need to go well beyond "modes of self-awareness" and talk about collective discursive practices, including legal and narrative practices that constitute us as persons. We will discuss this in the closing chapters of this book, and we will see that one will never find a self in such practices. The important point here is that when we talk about our immediate sense of self, our atavistic sense of who we are, we do *not* take ourselves to be constructed, or conventional, or to be "made out of different modes of self-awareness." That is the elephant. We take ourselves to be independent subjects and agents lying behind all of that. And that self-grasping can't be rendered innocuous by changing our terminology and focusing on personal identity instead of the reality of the self.

As I noted in chapter 1, Tsongkhapa calls our attention to two different kinds of self-grasping: self-grasping due to bad philosophy, and innate self-grasping. The first kind is theoretical and reflective; the second is instinctive. He claims that the first kind occurs when philosophers attempt to make sense of the illusion of the self by developing theories about its nature. This is a bit like seeing a mirage and then developing a theory to explain why there is a pond over there, one that will tell us just how much water it contains. The best way to deal with bad philosophy, he says, is to refute it using good philosophy. And that is what I have been trying to do in this chapter.

Innate self-grasping is harder. That powerful conviction that we are really selves arises not through careful reasoning, like that we have been discussing in this chapter, but instead because the illusion is so irresistible. We simply feel like selves. That is like seeing the mirage. No matter how much reasoning one offers a desert traveler, and no matter how much that person accepts that the experience is illusory, the experience and the illusion persist. The only way to eliminate that pre-reflective sense that there must be water there is to put on polarizing sunglasses: that is, to effect a deep transformation in the way we perceive the world.

Tsongkhapa's advice is that only long-term meditative exercise is capable of ridding us of the innate sense of self: it is too wired into our psyche to be extirpated just by doing philosophy. This is indeed one of the reasons that meditative practice is so important in Buddhist traditions: it is a vehicle through which philosophy can be transformative, by allowing that philosophy to seep so deeply into our consciousness that it comes to shape our experience. I conclude this chapter with that thought partly so that a reader who follows the arguments against the reality of the self but still feels the pull of the opposing position can see why that might be the case.

But I also end this chapter with this reflection because I think that Tsongkhapa might have been a little too pessimistic. I agree with him that a transformation of vision is necessary to see beyond the self illusion. But it just might be that that transformation can be achieved by closer attention to the times when that illusion is weakened or disappears. It is to those occasions that we now turn.

6

Immersion

SELFLESS SPONTANEITY AND SKILLFUL LIVING

SO FAR, we have been emphasizing the degree to which the illusion of self is natural and almost unavoidable. But this does not mean that we succumb to that illusion at every waking moment. There are times—perhaps more than we realize—when we don't represent ourselves as selves at all, when we spontaneously engage with the world in ways that implicate no sense of self. And indeed, these may be the most pleasant and rewarding moments of our lives. In this chapter, I will consider those spontaneous moments of selflessness, and what they suggest about who we are and about who we can aspire to become.

In order to get our minds around the experience of selflessness, it is useful to recall the deep connection between the sense of self, the understanding of experience in terms of subject-object duality, and of action in terms of free agency. To take ourselves to be selves, as we saw in chapter 1, is to take ourselves to be subjects with a very different mode of existence than that we assign to our objects. It is to regard ourselves as standing *against* the world rather than as being embedded *in* it. And it is to take our self-knowledge to be immediate, as opposed to the mediated knowledge we have of our objects.

Each of these modes of self-awareness is an aspect of subject-object duality, of taking experience to be a relation between these two entities of entirely different kinds. That polarity of subject and object in our experience is tantamount to the reification of a self. So, to the extent that we have experiences that are nondual in character, we are experiencing ourselves without positing a self.

We can make the same point about agency. To see ourselves as selves is to see ourselves as free agents acting upon the world, capable of agent causation that initiates actions on motives, actions whose causes lie entirely within us. This is how we often make sense of the difference between *action* and *mere behavior*, and this is how we often make sense of moral and legal responsibility. This is how subject-object duality looks in the domain of action. In perceptual experience the subject is divorced from the world and located as a spectator of it. By analogy, in action the agent is divorced from the causal nexus and acts freely upon it. Once again, then, to the extent that we experience ourselves as fully immersed, and not as freely initiating actions directed upon objects, our agency is nondual in character: we act without superimposing the self or the duality between self and other implicated by the sense of causally independent agency.

A Daoist Perspective

Up to this point, when drawing on Asian ideas, I have focused on those of Indian Buddhists and their interlocutors. But this is not the only Asian context in which we find deep reflection on the question of the reality of the self. We also find discussions of this kind of nondual, immersed awareness and agency in the Daoist as well as in the Chan and Zen Buddhist traditions. Let us begin with a justly famous passage from the Chinese classic the *Zhuangzi*: the story of Butcher Ding, a story that illustrates nonduality and selflessness both in the domain of subjectivity and in the domain of philosophy.

Butcher Ding was cutting up an ox for Lord Wenhui. At every touch of his hand, every heave of his shoulder, every move of his feet, every thrust of his knee—zip! zoop! He slithered the knife along with a zing, and all was in perfect rhythm, as though he were performing the dance of the Mulberry Grove or keeping time to the Ching-shou music.

"Ah, this is marvelous!" said Lord Wenhui. "Imagine skill reaching such heights!"

Butcher Ding laid down his knife and replied, "What I care about is the Way, which goes beyond skill. When I first began cutting up oxen, all I could see was the ox itself. After three years I no longer saw the whole ox. And now—now I go at it by spirit and don't look with my eyes. Perception and understanding have come to a stop and spirit moves where it wants. I go along with the natural makeup, strike in the big hollows, guide the knife through the big openings, and following things as they are. So I never touch the smallest ligament or tendon, much less a main joint.

"A good butcher changes his knife once a year—because he cuts. A mediocre Butcher changes his knife once a month—because he hacks. I've had this knife of mine for nineteen years and I've cut up thousands of oxen with it, and yet the blade is as good as though it had just come from the grindstone. There are spaces between the joints, and the blade of the knife has really no thickness. If you insert what has no thickness into such spaces, then there's plenty of room—more than enough for the blade to play about it. That's why after nineteen years the blade of my knife is still as good as when it first came from the grindstone.

"However, whenever I come to a complicated place, I size up the difficulties, tell myself to watch out and be careful, keep my eyes on what I'm doing, work very slowly, and move the knife with the greatest subtlety, until—flop! the whole thing comes apart like a clod of earth crumbling to the ground. I stand there holding the knife and look all around me, completely satisfied and reluctant to move on, and then I wipe off the knife and put it away."

"Excellent!" said Lord Wenhui. "I have heard the words of Butcher Ding and learned how to care for life!"[1]

There are a few things to note in this story. First, and most obviously, it is a story about skill acquisition, expertise, and the transformation of subjectivity as one moves from novice to virtuoso status in a domain. When he begins carving oxen, the butcher sees only oxen. This kind of perception, the kind we experience in much of our lives, presents objects to us. Inasmuch as it does, this kind of perceptual experience invites us to see ourselves as the subjects to whom those objects are presented, and to take ourselves to be distinct and removed from all of our objects of knowledge. In this mode of awareness, we experience ourselves as *selves*. As he matures in his skill, the oxen disappear, but Butcher Ding now sees their parts. His perception at this point in his development is more sophisticated, more nuanced, but still presents subject and object as distinct, and so continues to implicate the experience of the self.

When true virtuosity is achieved, though, "perception and understanding have come to a stop," and Ding cuts with "pure spirit." This may sound mystical, but it is not. And it should be familiar to anyone who has developed a complex perceptual-motor skill set, such as a musical or an athletic skill, or a skill in a martial art. These—like ox-butchering—are domains in which improvisation is necessary, and in which one must be able to perceive and to act with great accuracy and responsiveness to one's environment at great speed, without the luxury of continuous reflection and calculation.

When performing as a virtuoso, one is in what psychologists call a "flow" state.[2] In such a state, one experiences one's action as spontaneous, not as planned or calculated; one's own body, cognitive states, and the objects around one are not objects of reflective awareness, even though in these moments one is perhaps more closely perceptually attuned to the world and to one's own actions than at any other time. There is, despite this exquisite attunement and control, no experience of subject-object duality, and no awareness of self. The achievement of real expertise, the *Zhuangzi* suggests through this parable, is in part the achievement of this kind of perceptual skill and perceptual-motor attunement. In the achievement of virtuosity, if this is right, we also see the *elimination* of one's sense of self.

There is another nice insight we can glean from this story. While Ding and Wenhui might appear to be the only important characters, there is one more: the knife that, although it hasn't been sharpened in nineteen years, is still so sharp that it finds the spaces in the joints and moves through them effortlessly. Zhuangzi is reminding us here that the boundaries of our embodiment are not necessarily those of our human bodies. The tools and equipment we use become part of us as persons. We experience this all the time. When we use a stick to probe a hole, we feel the hole through the stick; when we drive a car, we experience the car as an extension of our body and feel ourselves to be in control of its movements; when we look into the rear-view mirror, we see not a reflection, but what is behind us, and so on. This reminds us of another aspect of the nonduality of our experience. We do not exist outside of our environment, perceiving it as subject, acting on it as agent; we are nondually immersed in it, with no clear boundary between ourselves and everything else.

This tale might appear to be anti-intellectual, or to suggest a complete abandonment of self-awareness. But that would be to read it incorrectly. The *Zhuangzi* does not mean to say that in achieving spontaneity, or selflessness, one gives up entirely on the ability to think and to calculate. As Ding says, "whenever I come to a complicated place, I size up the difficulties, tell myself to watch out and be careful, keep my eyes on what I'm doing, work very slowly, and move the knife with the greatest subtlety. . . ." I think that this is the most important moment in this parable, although it is easy to overlook. Careful, calculating thought can also, the *Zhuangzi* suggests, be spontaneous, and can be conducted without positing a self. We can become absorbed in thought, in solving a problem, or in a complex conversation or debate just as easily as we can become absorbed in carving an ox.[3]

And what goes for butchery goes for surgery. Zhuangzi's account of the role of *slowing down* and the processes that govern it are confirmed in recent studies of the attentional processes of skilled surgeons. Surgical skills, like sport skills—to which we will turn next—and highly trained expert skills in general, become highly automatized as surgeons acquire expertise, and experienced surgeons can perform complex tasks while conversing or listening to music.[4]

But in surgery, just as in butchery, complications sometimes arise that require the surgeon to slow down, and to transfer control from automated processing to careful, attentive cognitive control. As Moulton and Epstein put it, "the ability to make this transition appropriately in clinical practice [is] the hallmark of expertise."[5] And, like Butcher Ding, surgeons report that the shift from one mode of control to the other is as automatic and effortless as suturing at the close of surgery: it is one more aspect of automated skill, the spontaneous deployment of higher-order thought, or thought directed on thought. Moreover, like Ding, even when their attention is fully controlled and no longer automated, that attention is completely absorbed in their task, not in their own agency.[6]

We hence see that it is not the presence of explicit thought that distinguishes ego-involved experience from ego-less experience. Instead, this distinction reflects the degree of immersion in activity and so the degree to which explicit awareness of oneself as standing outside that activity is diminished. It is a distinction that is more phenomenological than psychological, having to do with how we experience our own engagement with the world. When we are completely immersed in activity—whether the physical activity of carving an ox or the cognitive activity of thinking about how best to carve that ox—our sense of self, and with it, the experience of the duality of subject and object in experience, vanish. There is only the experience of a flow of activity.

And this is a good thing for at least two reasons. First, immersed phenomenology is less likely to lead us into the error of positing the self. This is because the subject-object duality that thematizes the self as the subject of experience or the agent of action is itself a misleading structural superimposition on experience, a superimposition absent in immersed experience. Second, immersed phenomenology is indicative of expertise, and facilitates more fluid, successful performance.

Note that neither this observation, nor the story in the *Zhuangzi,* nor the experience of great surgeons, entail that non-immersed consciousness or calculative thought is always a *bad* thing. In fact, they tell us that it is often necessary. Note that Butcher Ding acknowledges that for years he saw only oxen or the parts of oxen, that is, that he carved oxen in a calculative rather than in an immersed way. This sounds like the dualistic mode of thought that implicates the distinction between subject and object, even though this is not how things would have been put in classical China. When we are learning, when we have not yet achieved expertise, or when we are teaching a skill to someone else and reflecting on it, it is often necessary to take this perspective on our activity.

This reflective, self-conscious perspective enables us to plan, to train, to monitor our own experience and actions so as to improve them. Skilled coaches direct us to monitor ourselves carefully while practicing a skill for this very reason. But they encourage this kind of explicit attention with the goal that we cast off that monitoring and awareness as we become more skilled. The point is that this kind of subjectivity has its point primarily in such circumstances, and it is useful primarily because of its power to facilitate immersed experience through the development of expertise. Self-monitoring is a *special,* not a *general* feature of our cognition, presupposing a background of fluid engagement with the world.

We are rarely aware of that omnipresent background of fluid engagement, a background necessary even for calculative, deliberate thought. After all, to make it an object of awareness would be to kill it. But if our awareness did not implicate this background—if it was always reflective and self-conscious—we could never function. We would always be caught up in a self-conscious obsession with our own present experiences, intentions, and actions, and like the proverbial centipede who was asked to explain how he coordinates all of those legs, we could no longer walk. But once we draw our attention to this background dimension of our psychology, we see that it is ubiquitous.

Sport psychology and the psychology of motor control more generally confirm these ideas. An ingenious study of the difference between the role of attention to a task in the process of skill acquisition and in expert performance shows that when novices are learning a skill, it is very important for them to attend to their own motor performance, and that anything that distracts attention from the task at hand inhibits performance. Novices who attend carefully to their own performance do much better at tasks such as putting in golf than do those who are distracted; self-conscious attention facilitates performance and learning.[7]

But once a skill is mastered, things change dramatically. Experts who are asked to attend to their own performance, unlike novices, do much *worse* than those who attend to a distractor, such as a conversation or music. And when experts "choke" under pressure, it is often excessive attention to themselves—in the guise either of their own performance or their own affective and cognitive states—that is the culprit. This is why sport psychologists working with expert athletes often prescribe listening to music or some other distractor to remove attention from oneself, and so to deal with this problem.

It is not that experts—whether athletes or surgeons—do not pay attention to what they are doing. Indeed, everyone who studies expert performance notes that one of the important dimensions of expertise is the development of skilled attention, including both the ability to attend to the right aspects of a situation and the ability to maintain focus. To be an expert football player is to be exquisitely aware of what the other players on the field are doing, of where they are, of where the ball is, etc. To be an expert surgeon is to be aware of countless relevant anatomical and physiological details. To be an expert typist is to be aware of what is being dictated. Expert awareness is far more highly tuned and specific than novice awareness in the same domain.

The point is rather that expert awareness differs from novice awareness in at least three important respects. First, it is directed principally outward, at goals, not reflexively, at action. This is so even though this expert awareness guides action through that goal-directedness. That is, the attention of the skilled batsman in cricket is on where he wants to hit the ball; the attention of the skilled surgeon is on the removal of the tumor. While the batsman's eyes are on the bowler, they shift unconsciously (saccade) with superb speed and accuracy to where the ball will strike the wicket. That is automatic. The batsman is focused on driving through covers. While the surgeon's eyes are fixed on the artery she is clamping, and while her fingers are involved in that intricate action, she is focused on the process of excision of the tumor.

Second, as the story of Ding reminds us, expert consciousness is nondual. The expert is not conscious of his or her own subjectivity and its relation to the object with which he or she is engaged, or even of the tools the expert might be using, including his or her own body. That is the kind of novice awareness that just gets in the way. Instead, the focused attention of the expert is entirely on the task at hand and on the goals to be accomplished through that task. It is immersed, embodied awareness, and awareness that is entirely fluid, adjusting to the ever-changing demands of the task at hand. Nothing resembling a self is ever present in this kind of consciousness. This is the sense in which actors or dancers, when they are successful, completely *inhabit* their roles, becoming the roles they embody, instead of experiencing *themselves* as performing those roles.[8]

Finally, skilled performance typically requires a fluidity, speed, and accuracy of movement, and a seamless integration of perception and action that would make such self-directed attention and deliberate planning impossible as a control mechanism. This phenomenon, to which researchers in motor control refer as *automaticity,* is most often studied in the context of domains such as sport or expert typing.[9] But we should not be distracted by this fact. What goes for batting in cricket, goaltending in football, or taking dictation in an office also goes for walking, conversation, and emotional engagement with another.

Applying the Daoist Insights, and a Bit of Zen

Why are these three characteristics of skilled performance so important for our purposes? For at least two reasons. First, we are at our best in expert performance. Expert performance reveals our most successful engagement with our world. The fact that this engagement is most successful when the self illusion is out of the picture is further evidence of the illusory status of the self. And the fact that such engagement takes the form of spontaneous interaction with the environment in which we are embedded shows that experiencing ourselves as persons is our most effective mode of being.

Second, however, and even more important, our intimate engagement with the world requires the constant deployment of this kind of expertise, which in turn requires that we shed the self illusion in favor of attunement to the world we inhabit. So, attention to what we take to be the self and to its activities— what we take to be self-awareness—has at best a limited utility, and even this explicit self-directed attention makes sense only in the context of a pervasive background of selfless attention to the world. We deploy our everyday human expertise constantly in walking, talking, reading, and engaging with friends and family. The same fluidity that the Olympic gymnast exhibits on the balance beam is exhibited as we maintain our balance while walking or riding a bicycle, or when we maintain our emotional balance when engrossed in an intimate conversation. Although this fact may escape our notice, in much of our life, our sense of self is absent. And that absence, as we can now see, is a good thing.

In one of his best-known essays, *Actualizing the Fundamental Point (Genjōkōan)*, the Zen philosopher Dōgen (1200–1253) writes,

> To study the self is to forget the self; to forget the self is to be actualized by the myriad things. When actualized by the myriad things, your body and mind as well as the bodies and minds of others drop away. No trace of realization remains, and this no-trace continues endlessly.[10]

Dōgen here connects the recognition of the absence of self with a kind of spontaneous engagement with reality, one that neither reifies subject and object nor consciously denies the reality of subject or object, but rather does not thematize subject and object at all.

Let us consider this passage with some care. "To study the self is to forget the self." That is, the more one understands one's own mode of existence, the more one understands that one is not a self. "To forget the self is to be actualized by the myriad things." To understand one's selflessness is to understand not that one is nonexistent, but that one is a real *person* in constant interaction with everything else in one's environment, a causally interdependent sequence of psychophysical processes. And it is to understand that the identity we do have—our personal identity—is not achieved alone, but instead is achieved only in immersed interaction with the rest of the world we inhabit. The myriad things—the entities of the empirical world—therefore do not constitute an independent reality with which we interact, but instead constitute our reality as sub-processes of the causal unfolding of the universe.

"When actualized by the myriad things, your body and mind as well as the bodies and minds of others drop away." This kind of spontaneous skillful interaction in the world results in the cessation of the reification of subject and object: one is not conscious of one's own body and mind as constituting a subjective pole of experience; nor is one aware of external phenomena as constituting an objective pole of experience. In spontaneous, virtuoso interaction, one simply interacts, with no bifurcation of the world into subject/object or agent/action/object. "No trace of realization remains, and this no-trace continues endlessly." This is not a positive awareness of selflessness, or a focus on nondual awareness; it is simply the absence of any reification of self, or dualistic consciousness, and an attitude that can become a permanent expert mode of being.

Dōgen, like Nāgasena, is not arguing for our unreality, and he is certainly not arguing that we have no experience. He is arguing instead that our reality is that of embedded persons, not that of independent selves. He is also arguing that even though we may sometimes superimpose a dualistic structure on our experience, and even take that for granted as the way we encounter the world, that duality is a superimposition on a primordially nondual mode of awareness. While it might sometimes be useful to think in dualistic terms, to do so without awareness of the artificial, cognitive origin of that structure is to fail in self-understanding.

All of this is to say that to take subject-object dualism to be a universal feature of awareness would be a serious overgeneralization: it would be to take a very special kind of cognition that is appropriate in very particular domains to be appropriate and present in all awareness. In those special moments in which we need to become aware of our own subjectivity, doing so can facilitate our engagement with the world. But in most cases, that superimposition does not render us more effective or more aware of what transpires around us. Instead, it makes us less aware of our surroundings and of the objects or others to whom we should be attending; that is, it makes us self-conscious in the pejorative sense of that term. This is why a good deal of martial arts training is dedicated to replacing calculative thought, dualistic appearance, and the thematization of self with nondual, spontaneous, selfless performance.

Heidegger has a nice way of putting this. He distinguishes between two different ways that the stuff of our world can show up for us in awareness. A thing may be part of my world in virtue of being *ready to hand* (*Zuhandenheit*) or it may be an object in my world in virtue of being *present to hand* (*Vorhandenheit*). When something is ready to hand, I don't notice it as an object, or stand to it as subject to object. It is very much a part of my immersed action, and not distinguished in awareness from me, the agent. As I am typing these words, my keyboard is like that: like Ding's knife, it is experienced as an extension of myself, a tool that is seamlessly integrated with my thinking and my fingers. My fingers are also ready to hand. I don't think of them as objects, but rather as part of my agency, again reflecting the porosity of the boundary between person and environment.

But suppose that something happens to my keyboard: the battery may go dead, or a key may stick. When that occurs, the keyboard suddenly becomes thematized as an object. It is present in my field of awareness, and no longer seamlessly integrated with me. Like Butcher Ding, I slow down, and carefully consider what I should to fix the situation. Note that the same thing may happen to my fingers (and it often does!). Tendonitis may set in. They hurt. They then cease to be a seamless part of my activity and they are objectified, alienated from me as subject, I take them as objects of my thought as I consider what to do about them.

The structure of subject-object duality emerges, on Heidegger's account, only in these situations where fluid, immersed, embedded, embodied perception and action in the world breaks down. That duality is not a pervasive aspect of our conscious lives, but a specific response to an abnormal situation. And just as in the Butcher Ding story, it does not signal the complete absence of fluid nondual awareness, or the emergence of the activity of a self, but rather a fluid, nondual engagement in a form of thought that itself projects a subject-object duality as a technique for coping with breakdown.

The fact that what we can say for the keyboard we can say as well for the fingers typing on it is also important. It is tempting to think that the fact of our embodiment means that our bodies form a kind of boundary between us and the world. That would be to infer fallaciously from the fact that we are embodied to the conclusion that we as persons are identical with our bodies, like inferring the identity of a real English actor and a fictional Danish prince from the fact that Cumberbatch is playing Hamlet.[11]

That would be to see things in terms of inner and outer, self and other, subject and object. It would therefore also be to forget that as persons we are not only embodied, but embedded. And just as our bodies can fall either on the subject or the object side of our awareness, the environment beyond our bodies can do so as well. We experience this when we type, when we write, when we drive, or when we ride a bicycle. When we are immersed in action, our conscious perspective includes that of the equipment through which we engage, just as a blind person experiences her point of contact with the world at the end of a cane. Keeping this in mind helps to reinforce the idea that the imagination of the self is context-specific, and always a construction, not a discovery.

7

Ethics

ABANDON THE SELF
TO ABANDON EGOISM

SO FAR, we have explored the sources of the idea that there is a self, and to refute that idea in favor of the view that we are selfless persons. This might seem like an interesting but idle philosophical exercise, but it is not idle at all. The theoretical rubber hits the human road when we turn to questions about ethics, and we will now see that the self illusion has moral dimensions.

When I represent the nature of my existence and the existence of others as that of a self among selves, my view of the moral landscape I inhabit is colored in ways that, although easy to take them for granted, can be pernicious. When I come to see myself as a person among persons, the moral landscape takes on very different hues, and my sense of agency, responsibility, and cultivation are transformed. Each way of seeing things results in a particular sense of agency and moral responsibility, a particular sense of what is *prima facie* motivational, a particular sense of our place in the moral landscape, and a particular sense of what moral cultivation and moral education should look like. Let us consider each of these in turn. But first,

I want to talk briefly about egoism, and what is wrong with it. Keeping that in focus will help us to address these other issues.

Moral Egoism

Moral egoism is the view that it is morally acceptable for me to act in my own narrow self-interest. Rational egoism is the somewhat weaker thesis that it is at least *prima facie* rational for me to act in my own narrow self-interest. Indeed, adherence to rational egoism is sometimes even taken as a criterion of rationality itself in domains such as game theory or economics. In much economic theory, it is presumed to operate as the motivating principle for rational competitors or participants in a market. Even that great proponent of the impartial viewpoint, the philosopher John Rawls (1921–2002), takes egoistic concern as the basis of rational deliberation in his magisterial account of justice.[1]

On this view, only extremely weighty considerations should ever override egoistic concern, and egoistic reasons are default justifiers for action. So, for instance, if someone asks me why I choose to invest my money in a high-yield but morally questionable fund, the assertion that I want to maximize my return is, on this view, a *prima facie* justification for my action. The fact that somebody might try to dissuade me from this course of action by pointing out its implications for my reputation indicates that even that person takes my immediate self-interest to be a rational justifier that demands a response.

Moral egoism strikes many of us immediately as unacceptable. The idea that what is morally correct is what is in my narrow self-interest undermines the very idea of moral reflection. Instead, moral reflection requires us to see our own interests as just some among many, and to take the interests of others as motivations for our actions as well—to recognize that there is nothing morally *special* about ourselves. The moral point of view, that is, is a disinterested point of view, the direct opposite of the self-interested point of view of egoism.[2]

We can put this point in terms of the structure of the moral landscape. Egoism is motivated by seeing ourselves at the center of that landscape, and then locating others on a kind of polar coordinate system by distance and direction from us. In the favorable hemisphere, our immediate family (for many of us) might be closest, followed by distant family and close friends. A bit further out are our colleagues, and then casual acquaintances. They in turn are surrounded by others we may not know, but with whom we identify, perhaps co-religionists, fans of the same cricket team, citizens of the same country. Still further out in the moral universe, things may get a bit homogenous, and blend into a kind of neutrality among concerns. On the negative side, we might first encounter those we detest—perhaps those who have harmed us, our loved ones, or our interests. Beyond them are those we find simply annoying, or with whom our interests conflict. And further out, we find fans of that other cricket side, or citizens of a country with whom ours is in conflict, and so forth.

When we see the world this way, we find a *prima facie* reason—proximity—to prefer our own interests to those of others, the interests of our family over those of our colleagues, theirs over other co-citizens, and so forth, and to prefer one hemisphere of associates to the other. We even find good reasons to act against the interests of those in the wrong pie slice of our particular moral universe. When we see the world this way, moral interest tracks location in relation to ourselves. We take pride of place not only as those whose interests we take to be paramount, but also as those on whom the moral value of everyone else depends. We are each the points of origin of our own moral universes.

When we describe this attitude so baldly, it seems preposterous for a number of reasons. For one thing, each of us has the same claim to the center of the moral universe, and we can't all occupy that spot. If I am at the center, you are in the periphery. If you are at the center, I am in the periphery. The fact that we each have equal claim to the center means that none of us has any claim to that position at all. For another, it makes moral standing conditional on my relations and attitudes towards you. But the very point of morality is to serve as a counterbalance to those very attitudes and relations. As Kant pointed out, if morality merely tracks my desires and preferences, it is no morality at all. We expect more impartiality—and more of a brake on desire from our moral reasoning—than that. Finally, it is a recipe for irresolvable moral conflict, as each of us has our moral demands specified by our particular version of the moral landscape. Morality, as Rawls so eloquently emphasizes, demands common assent.

Nonetheless, despite the manifest absurdity of this vision of the moral universe, it is—at least implicitly, if rarely explicitly—widely shared. We appeal to this version of moral geography every time we prefer our own interests over those of others, and every time we decide that someone is not worthy of our consideration because they fall into an out-group, or because they have in some way harmed us. We do so when we take it to be natural for me to prefer the interests of my family to those of yours. When we take these attitudes for granted as justifiable, we implicitly relativize our moral judgments to our own situation; we center ourselves in the moral universe.

This common, even instinctive, tendency is the moral coun-
terpart and consequence of the view that we are selves. This is
because it re-reinscribes the subject-object distinction that
originates as an account of our *cognitive* relation to the world,
but this time as an account of our *ethical* relation to the world.
To see everything through the subject-object lens is to see oneself as subject and agent, and everyone else as moral objects and
as patients. Only this instinctive attitude can provide any motivation at all for this way of thinking about ethical life. And this
is one more problem with the attitude that we are selves. When
we ascribe that kind of independence, separation from the
world in which we act, and immediate intimacy to ourselves, it
is a very short step to moral egoism.

A Selfless Moral Landscape: The *Brahmavihāras*

What is the alternative? Well, we already know that on the metaphysical side, the alternative to understanding our mode of existence as that of selves is to understand ourselves as persons—
as beings who come into existence in open causal interaction
with the rest of the world, and whose identity is constituted by
the collectively composed narrative in which we are *dramatis
personae*. To see oneself that way is to locate oneself in a decen-
tered universe, with no special moral point of origin, and in
which one's own location is no more special than that of anyone
else. That is to see oneself as a character in a play with no special
protagonists, a play performed and written on the fly by a vast
improv collective. This universe, unlike the one that motivates
egoism, gives one no reason for special self-regard, or to distinguish between the moral standing of others in virtue of their
relationships to oneself.

To understand the moral implications of this divergent vision of the moral landscape, it is useful to turn to Buddhist ethical thought for inspiration, for much of that moral thought— especially that of Śāntideva, of the Dalai Lama XIV, and of Thich Nhat Hanh—is inspired by reflections on selflessness such as these.[3] The ideas that we will discover, although first articulated within that tradition, are immediately recognizable as rational moral responses to the world we inhabit. They are summarized in Buddhist theory under the four *divine states (brahmavihāras)* as *friendliness, care, sympathetic joy,* and *impartiality.* Let us first consider each of them individually and then turn to the moral vision they collectively reflect and induce. Each emerges from an understanding of our interdependence with those around us, and of our joint participation in the world we share.

An attitude of friendliness is one in which we wish well for others and strive to benefit them. It is an attitude of wishing well for their sake, not because their happiness gives us any particular pleasure. That is to say, it is a disinterested benevolence. It must therefore be distinguished not only from its obvious antithesis—hostility—but also from what the Indian Buddhist philosopher Buddhaghosa (c. 370–450 CE) felicitously calls its *near enemy*, partial affection. To adopt this latter attitude—in which one is a good friend to those one likes, but not to others, or in which one's motivation for wishing for another's good is because it is pleasant for oneself—might feel good, and might even feel like being a good friend. But it would be to reinscribe the egocentric understanding of the moral world to which this alternative vision is meant to be an antidote.

Just as to be friendly is to wish for good things for others, to be caring is to act to alleviate others' pain and suffering. It is to wish to alleviate it just because it is suffering, not because of the other's relationship to oneself, and not because of how that suffering affects oneself. That is, like true friendliness, true care is disinterested. And so, like friendliness, it must be distinguished both from its antithesis—callousness—and from its near enemy, pity, or sloppy sympathy.[4] When we respond to another's suffering with pity or sympathy, we suffer a contagion of suffering, and consequently are impaired in our ability to act with real care. You don't want your surgeon to *feel* your pain, but to *care* for you, unimpaired by that pain. Care thus requires and reinforces a non-egocentric view of the world, a view of the world as a place we inhabit as persons, not against which we stand as selves.

Sympathetic joy is the ability to take pleasure in the success of others. It is the antithesis of *schadenfreude*. And once again, distinguishing it from its near enemy allows us to understand the way in which it both emerges from and constitutes a non-egocentric comportment to the world. The near enemy in this case is partiality, or jingoism. This is the attitude in which we rejoice in the success of those with whom we associate, or those who we take to be our friends, or to be "on our side," while being indifferent to or even dismayed by the success of those we perceive as more distant from us in the moral landscape. Once again, that is an attitude that takes our own location to be special, and that assigns degrees of moral concern to others in terms of their proximity to us. That assignment of a special role to ourselves at the moral origin is part of the self illusion, and sympathetic joy is inconsistent with that orientation.

This brings us naturally to the fourth of these characteristics, impartiality. That is an attitude that we can now see both as important on its own and also in virtue of the fact that it informs and is reflected in the three attitudes we have just discussed. To be impartial is to adopt the same moral attitude, and to extend the same level of friendship, care, and sympathetic joy to all in one's environment, regardless of their relation to oneself, regardless of whether one sees them as close to one, or distant, supportive or hostile. It is to forego both revenge and partiality. It is not a refusal of affection or goodwill to one's intimates, but to be willing to extend that natural fellow-feeling indefinitely, and so to assign a kind of homogeneity to the moral world.

Together these attitudes are valorized as *divine* in the Buddhist tradition. This is because they encapsulate a complete abandonment of egocentricity in moral experience. The egocentricity they undermine is the moral side of regarding oneself as *a self,* which we now understand as the implicit view that one's own status is different from that of the rest of the world and that the status of others is dependent on their relation to oneself. To see things from the egocentric perspective reflecting the view of a self is to remove oneself from *membership* in the world and to adopt the position of an *experiencer* of the world and an *agent* acting on it. And that is the moral side of the self illusion. Its inevitable consequence is—at best—the adoption of the near enemies of these four virtuous states as one's mode of comportment, substituting rationally defensible, beneficial attitudes with irrational and ultimately destructive ones, made all the worse because they can masquerade so effectively as virtue.[5]

To the extent that we recognize these divine states as constituting a moral ideal, and as reflections of a rational way to understand our own place in the moral world, we see that it is both rational and morally important to shed the self illusion. It is rational to do so because it fails to fit our best understanding of the world and our place in it. It is morally important, because this investigation reveals that the self illusion is not harmless. And in the end, it issues in pernicious attitudes that make us less effective and less beneficial moral agents, attitudes that we cannot help but recognize as pathological.[6]

A Selfless Moral Landscape: Agency

Śāntideva, in chapter 6 of *How to Lead an Awakened Life*, points out that the self illusion has other serious moral implications. In particular, he argues, it leads to unwarranted attributions of free agency to ourselves and to others. This in turn leads to unjustified pride and anger, as well as to indefensible egoism. By freeing ourselves from the illusion that we and others are selves, he urges, we get a clearer vision of what propels action, we reduce anger, we better modulate our own affective lives, and we become more caring. Let us examine his arguments for these conclusions.

Why is the illusion of the self so deeply connected to the illusion of absolute freedom, or of agent causation? When we think of ourselves as persons, we think of ourselves as continua of psychophysical processes, and we are generally pretty comfortable thinking of every mental or physical event we identify as ours as having causes. My raising my arm is caused by my intention to do so. That intention is caused by my desire to get the waiter's attention. That desire in turn is caused by my belief that if I don't, he won't bring me dessert, as well as by my desire for dessert. And my belief that he is on the way is caused by my current perceptions and my memory of what he looks like, and so on.

When we recognize that we are part of the causal order, the fact that all of our perceptions, thoughts, and actions are *caused* seems just obvious. It then appears bizarre to think, or to wish, that our behavior is *uncaused*. To be uncaused would be to be *random*; and to behave randomly would not be a kind of freedom, but instead a terrible curse, leaving us no control over any aspect of our lives.

But we are not entirely consistent in the ways we think about ourselves, and this view of ourselves as immersed in the causal nexus is not our only self-understanding. When we deliberate about what to do, or when we assign blame or praise to ourselves or others, we often instinctively do so on the assumption that our—or their—actions are not caused by previous events. Instead, we pre-reflectively take our actions, as well as those of others, to be the result of what gets called "agent causation," a spontaneous act of the will unconstrained by deterministic causes. So, if I become annoyed because you push me from behind, you might mollify me by pointing out that you did not voluntarily push me, but were yourself pushed into me by the person behind you. Knowing that your motion was caused and not a free action reduces the likelihood that I will blame you for it.

The idea that there is this special kind of causation is enshrined not only in our cognitive habits, but also in the law. So, for instance, when you go to a notary public to have a signature notarized, you will be asked, "Is this your free act and deed?" or words to that effect. And in criminal cases, demonstrating that an act was *caused* rather than *freely chosen* can be exculpatory. The insanity defense, or a defense that appeals to coercion, would be an example of this kind of thinking. In each case, we assign responsibility when we take an action to have been free, and so we withdraw assignment of responsibility when we see that action to have been caused. This is the kind of freedom that could only be enjoyed by a transcendent self.

In Western philosophy, this tendency to draw the contrast between free acts and acts that are caused—a distinction that motivates debates about the freedom of the will—has its roots in the work of the philosopher Augustine of Hippo (354– 430 CE). He introduced the idea in order to absolve God of moral responsibility for the fall of Adam and Eve in the Garden of Eden. Augustine was worried that if God is really omnipotent, omnibenevolent, and omniscient, as Church doctrine would have it, then he could have prevented Adam and Eve from sinning. Since he didn't, he reasoned, one might then hold God morally responsible for their eating the proverbial apple; if so, it would have been wrong of God to punish them by expelling them from the Garden.

Augustine solved this theological conundrum by introducing the idea of a free will. Note that this required him to introduce *two* new ideas: that of a *will*, and that of its exemption from causation. The will was introduced as a *faculty*: a tool at our disposal, the general ability to initiate action. The idea that it is *free* is the idea that when we deploy this will, there is no antecedent cause for our volition. We simply initiate the action on our own, intervening in the causal order from the outside, so to speak.

We can see how this invention gets God off the hook. Since Adam and Eve acted freely, even if God knew about their plans, and even if God really wished that they wouldn't act on them, their freedom set a limit on his omnipotence: He could only have prevented them from acting if those actions were caused. But since they weren't, the fault lies not with God but with Adam and Eve. So, out of a theological problem, a moral, legal, and metaphysical ideology was born. And this ideology has become so deeply ingrained in our culture that we accept it without question. We forget its religious roots and motivation—roots and motivation we might want to think twice about endorsing.

Why, you might ask, are we following this theological byway? For the following reason: this sense of special freedom from the causal nexus and the idea that we are selves are tightly linked to one another. This is because to think of oneself as a person is, as I have been emphasizing, to think of oneself as a continuum of causally connected psychophysical processes in open causal interaction with the rest of the world in which one is embedded. There is no room for Augustinian agent causation here.

The events that make up our own continua are no different from any other events with respect to whether they are caused or not.

To think of oneself as standing outside of causality, on the other hand, is effectively to think of oneself as a special kind of entity that acts on the causal nexus, but which is not constrained by it. That is the kind of autonomy and distinction from the world, including our own bodies and minds, that we ascribe to a self, and when you think about it, it doesn't make all that much sense. Moreover, the self-instinct and the free will instinct are hence two sides of the same coin.[7]

And this is one more reason that it is so morally problematic to posit a self. When we do so, we forget that the actions of others are not free in the Augustinian sense, but caused. An act that is harmful to me may, Śāntideva argues, be caused by pathologies that are as painful to the actor as the actions are to me, pathologies that are hardly chosen by that agent. Here is how he puts it in *How to Lead an Awakened Life*:

6.22　When I don't get angry
　　　With sources of great suffering such as jaundice,
　　　Then why get angry with sentient beings?
　　　They are also propelled by conditions.

6.23　Consider this: although nobody wants them,
　　　Illnesses like jaundice befall us.
　　　Just so, although nobody wants them,
　　　Our psychopathologies inevitably befall us.

6.24　Just as nobody ever thinks, "Let me now come
　　　　　into existence."
　　　Nobody ever thinks, "Now let me be angry."
　　　Instead, people just get angry.
　　　That is just how anger occurs.

6.25 All of our errors
       And all of the various kinds of evil
       Arise through the force of conditions:
       None of them are autonomous.

6.31 Thus everything depends on something else.
       And that on which it depends is never independent.
       Knowing this, one should never be angry
       At things that are like magical illusions.

6.33 So, when one sees anyone—whether friend or foe—
       Perform an unreasonable action,
       One can think, "this has been brought about by
         conditions,"
       And so one can remain content.

6.41 If I am injured by something such as a stick,
       And I get angry with the person who wields it,
       Then, since he is in turn impelled by aversion,
       It would make more sense for me to be angry at
         that aversion.

6.43 His knife and my body
       Are the two causes of my suffering.
       Since he holds the knife and I my body,
       At which should I be angry?[8]

So, it might be more appropriate and more effective for me to respond to harmful actions with an attitude of care—a commitment to help that person to escape from the emotional state or the beliefs that caused their harmful action—than with an attitude of blame. This is because anger only inspires a desire to cause them further harm. I might note that my own morally problematic actions are similarly often caused by pathologies that I do not willingly endure. I might therefore conclude that it would be better for me to respond to those pathologies by seeking help than by wallowing in guilt. Self-satisfaction as I contemplate actions of which I am proud might well turn to gratitude towards others and a bit of humility when I recognize that the causes of those actions may lie well outside myself, and gratitude and humility might in the end be more salutary reactions than pride.[9]

Our moral attitudes and our moral development are hence bound up with our view of our own natures and the natures of those around us. Seeing ourselves as autonomous selves among other autonomous selves both gets the nature of agency wrong and lead us to maladaptive behavior and attitudes. Seeing ourselves as persons in an interdependent matrix of other persons both gives us greater insight into our own and others' agency and leads us to healthier moral responses and greater moral maturity. To put this another way, who we think we are determines in part who we eventually become.[10]

And this is one very important reason to take the self illusion seriously. It is not a harmless illusion, like the Müller-Lyer. It is more like a mirage seen by a desperately thirsty traveler lost in the desert that takes the traveler deeper into the waterless waste and further from genuine succor. When we see ourselves as selves, genuine moral engagement is blocked; when we see ourselves as persons, it is enabled. Another reason to take the self illusion seriously is that so long as we are bound by it, we fail to see clearly who and what we are, and in what the meaning of our lives consists. It is to those issues that we now turn.

8

Affirmation

BECOMING AND BEING A PERSON
AMONG PERSONS

SO FAR, we have talked more about what we *aren't* than about what we *are* and how we get to be that way. In these final chapters, we will focus on just what a person *is*, how persons are constituted, and how we *become* persons. The discussion will be philosophical, but grounded in what evolutionary theory, social science, and psychology tell us about who and what we are. Persons are poised between the biological, the psychological, and the social, and they live on the cusp of fact and fiction.

Exploring the mode of reality of persons forces us to confront these two axes of analysis. This requires us to attend to multiple dimensions of our existence, and to reflect on what kinds of beings are produced by and in turn produce the world in which we are embedded. While the discussion may sometimes seem to stray from the topic of the nature of persons opposed to selves, it is worth following the swings and roundabouts, as in the end we will see that it is only by understanding ourselves as persons that we can really understand what it is for life to be meaningful. Let us begin by talking about fact and fiction, as some of what I will have to say may call this apparent contrast into question.

Fact and Fiction

As we noted in chapter 3, the words *fact* and *fiction* are cognate in English, deriving from the Latin *fingere,* which means *to make. Fact* is thus closely related to *factory,* a place where things are made; *fictions* are things we make up. So, each term has the connotation of something constructed, something artificial, but nonetheless real in some sense. It is now time to explore with more care the idea that to be fictional is not necessarily to be unreal. As we saw in that context, fictions may constitute facts. Let us consider two kinds of examples of how this comes about before turning more directly to persons.

Recall first that in a literary fiction none of the characters are real outside the scope of the text. But we also saw that although the characters are all manufactured by their authors, to manufacture is to make facts, and sometimes, even in the case of literary fiction, those facts transcend the literary work itself. It is true, for instance, that Rosencrantz and Guildenstern were executed in Norway, and false that Hamlet was. It is even true that Rosencrantz and Guildenstern are characters both in *Hamlet* and in Tom Stoppard's *Rosencrantz and Guildenstern Are Dead,* a fact that Shakespeare could not have created, and a truth he could not have known. Fictional characters, that is, may escape the control of their creators and take on lives of their own. Moreover, even in the case of literary fictions there are facts of the matter, and as we noted in chapter 3, a real difference between truth and falsehood is as good a criterion of reality as any.

Let us now consider a fiction of a different kind: the fiction that underlies the value of money, an example we introduced earlier in a different context. Consider a $20 banknote and a $1 banknote. The paper and ink that constitute them have no real intrinsic value, and the paper and the ink in the $20 note are certainly not twenty times the value of that in the $1 banknote. The value of each note is entirely manufactured by the United States banking system, and the marketplace in which it is accepted. The value of the notes depends upon the willingness of others to accept them in exchange, which depends in turn on what we tell each other about such things.[1] If we stopped treating these pieces of paper as valuable, they would lose all value. They are effectively characters in a collectively narrated fiction.

That fact, however, does not make these banknotes any less valuable, nor does it mean that money in general is any less real. It only reminds us that the reality of banknotes as money is constituted by and has no reality outside of a set of stories we tell. Money and the value of banknotes are not part of the fundamental or primordial world; they do not exist prior to our human practices and conventions, awaiting our discovery; we created them. In this respect, they are just like Hamlet, Ophelia, Rosencrantz, and Guildenstern.

But money and its value, unlike those Shakespearean characters, are definitely real in another sense. Exploring this sense shows us that fictional facticity is not an oxymoron, but rather the mode of existence of many of the entities that constitute our world. It is the mode of existence shared by nations, corporations, clubs, and baseball games. What could be more real than these everyday objects? This is what Buddhist philosophers like Candrakīrti have in mind when they characterize this kind of reality as *conventional (samvṛti),* or as *determined by mundane transactions (lokavyāvahāra).* And this is why conventional or mundane transactional existence is not *second-class* existence: in the end, this is what it is to exist at all.

I belabor this point because I am trying to convince you that this is the kind of reality that persons enjoy. We are fictional, but also factual. We are brought into existence as persons through the complex interplay between our biology as members of species *Homo sapiens* and our interactions with one another in the context of the social structures that make persons both possible and necessary. That origin renders us fictional, or constructed; it means that our reality as persons is not primordial, or independent of human activity. But this tale of origins does not render us *unreal.* Persons are also factual. We, like the civilizations, cities, and civic practices we create, are real parts of the natural and social world. And we have real biological, psychological, and social properties. That is what genuine, empirical reality is; the kind of supernatural reality that would attach to a self is no reality at all.

Many Levels

To understand what it is to be a person in this sense requires us to understand the complex interplay between the many levels of analysis in which we turn up. It may be tempting to think that these are hierarchical: that biology is the most fundamental and important way to understand our existence (or even the physics and chemistry that might be thought to ground that level), and that all of the other levels at which we understand ourselves are derivative of these physical levels. If you succumb to this temptation, you might then think that psychology is next, and that it can be ultimately understood as a mere manifestation of our biology, prominently including our neurobiology. And then you might think that the social sciences ride on top of that. Social and behavioral science are, on this view, what you do until the biologist comes. And to think this way is to think that persons are fundamentally biological entities.[2]

This is the wrong way to look at things, and the wrong way to understand our identity as persons. It betrays a faith in reductionism that is not warranted. Before explaining what is wrong with that idea, and before offering an alternative, I want to spend a moment on the kernel of truth in it, if only to disarm resistance to an alternative way of seeing things. The kernel of truth is the idea of *supervenience*. This is a technical term in philosophy, but it is easy to understand. In brief, to say that one level of description (the supervening level) supervenes on another (the base level) is just to say that any two worlds where everything is the same at the base level are also identical at the supervening level.

A game of chess, for instance, supervenes on the movements of chess pieces on a board. This just means that in any two worlds where the same movements of pieces are made on the chessboard (and the same conventions are operative), the same chess games are played. The amount of money in my wallet supervenes on the physical objects in my wallet. Anybody with the same banknotes in their wallet has just as much money as I do. Supervenience in this sense captures the idea that facts at some levels of description determine those at others, even if they don't do so piecemeal, and even if it is impossible to replace one level with another.

But the supervenience of chess on the physical is consistent with the fact that that same chess game could have been played online, with nothing moving around on a physical board. Chess moves are therefore neither identical with nor reducible to the movements of wooden pieces on a board, even though they may be instantiated by those movements. Nor could we replace a theory of chess with a theory of wooden objects and their movements. The money in my wallet, as we have seen, is neither identical with nor reducible to the banknotes, even though they instantiate it. There are plenty of other ways to have that much money.

So, to say that one level of description supervenes on another is not to say that the first is reducible to that other, or that it can be replaced, but only that if we fix all of the facts at the base level, we would thereby have fixed all of the facts at the supervening level.[3] The kernel of truth in the intuition that the biological is more fundamental than the psychological, and that the psychological is more fundamental than the social, is that this is the general direction of supervenience relations.[4]

We can accept that idea without thinking that the base levels can ever replace the supervening levels, and without thinking that the base levels explain everything about the supervening levels. You can't use physics to understand a chess game, or to understand how money works. You need to know how to play chess to understand a chess game, since it is the same game whether it is played with wooden pieces or online. You need to know some economics to understand money; it can be passed around either as cash or electronically.

Most importantly, although a bit harder to see, we need to resist the thought that we can always understand what goes on at the base levels without attention to the supervening levels. That is, some aspects of our biology are driven by our psychology and our social structures; some aspects of our psychology are driven by our social matrix as well. So, to understand who and what we are, all of these levels of description—and maybe more—are necessary. This is not a new idea. It was made eloquently by the psychologist Edward Chace Tolman (1886–1959):

I would define physiology as a study of the laws determining the *activities* of muscles and glands; I would define psychology as a study of the laws determining the *behavior* of whole organisms; and I would define sociology as the study of the laws determining the *conduct* of groups of organisms. Accepting these definitions, one's first reaction concerning the interrelations of the three sciences would be to think of physiology as the most basic, psychology as the next most basic, and sociology as the least basic—or, in other words, to conceive the facts and laws of psychology as dependent upon those of physiology and the facts and laws of sociology as dependent upon those of psychology. But the thesis that I am actually going to try to uphold here is the reverse and, at first sight, seemingly absurd one, to wit: that the facts and laws of psychology are, rather, in some part dependent upon those of sociology and that the facts and laws of physiology are similarly in some part dependent upon those of psychology.[5]

We are an ultrasocial species. We are genetically programmed for social interactions of all kinds, including parent-child interactions, language learning, friendship, etc. There is nothing controversial about this. Now let's think about the impact of this ultrasociality on who we have become. That sociality has allowed us to evolve into language users, into beings who construct and inhabit complex societies with intricate political, economic, and social structures. That is, over hundreds of generations, we have collectively engineered the niche we inhabit.

That niche, in turn, constitutes the context in which we are selected and in which we evolve, and the context in which our psychology is shaped. So, for instance, once the broad outlines of our linguistic, sociopolitical, and economic regime are in place, our psychology responds to those demands. We learn to think and even to introspect, and so to know ourselves, in the languages we speak.[6] The metaphors, semantic distinctions, and even the syntax and orthography of our languages shape our thought and our perception of the world, including what color distinctions we draw, or how we experience and understand time.[7]

The political and economic conditions that determine social success or failure, the material conditions of the work we do, and the spaces we inhabit also shape our preferences. These conditions also determine what is salient to us in our environment, our range of options for action, what information we acquire, and how we deploy that information in reasoning and in planning our lives. In short, how we think, what our goals are, how we behave, and what gives us pleasure and pain are to a large part determined by our social context. It is therefore impossible to understand who we are psychologically without understanding who we are socially.

Tolman offers the example of trying to understand the behavior (and, we might add, the affect and thought) of a bridegroom at his wedding. The bridegroom will do many things, feel many things, and think many thoughts. Most of those actions and psychological states will reflect in some way the social construction of marriage and the marriage ceremony in his culture, the views and practices of his family or of his co-religionists, etc., and perhaps his own social and economic standing. It is impossible to predict, to explain, or to understand his psychology without understanding the social context in which he plays the role (the *persona*) of a bridegroom, and his larger role—the person he is—in the social drama in which he is embedded. His physical behavior (say, slipping a ring on a woman's finger) can only be explained psychologically and socially; his physical expression of emotion makes sense only in the context of a cul-ture that thematizes romantic love.[8] Once one sees this point, one sees that this is true regarding almost all of our psychology. The lines we speak, the gestures we make, the lives we lead, are structured in large part by the roles we play and the social struc-tures that define those roles and make them possible.

Of course, there are also important biological constraints on our thought and behavior. One can only perform on the stage what one is biologically capable of doing. Our sensory appara-tus, nervous system, and musculature help to explain how we see, move, and interact with one another. These constraints are independent of, but interact with, the stage directions an actor receives and the script they follow. But these factors are not sufficient to explain what the actor does. To provide a complete explanation, one must refer to the play in which he is perform-ing, the director's conception of that play, the culture of the theatre, etc. Similarly, the bridegroom's behavior is constrained by and partly explained by his biology, and biology interacts with social variables to determine how he perceives, moves, and reacts. Despite this fact, his biology is insufficient to explain much of what transpires at his wedding: a lot of biography and social theory is necessary as well.

Moreover, even our biological nature and processes can often be understood only with reference to our psychology and social context. The bridegroom may sweat, or shake. His blood pressure may rise. His pupils may contract. To be sure, these are biological processes, each of which can be explained in some sense by appealing to straightforwardly biological causes. Nonetheless, we see in an instant that to explain or to under-stand these processes, we must appeal both to the bridegroom's psychology and to the social structures that generate his anxiety and excitement. Biology alone would tell us very little about what is going on; we therefore need the social level of explanation even to understand the biological facts on which that social level supervenes. The explanation and understanding of the behavior of persons are two-way streets.

There is an evolutionary point here as well. As biological organisms, we are subject to selection pressures. Each of us exists only because our parents survived to reproduce. The fact that we lived to adulthood, perhaps to reproduce ourselves, required that many others in our community survived as well, and were willing to cooperate with us. Those who do survive pass the genes that enabled them to do so to their offspring. The social and psychological complexity of the niche we inhabit—a niche that can only be understood in those social and psychological terms—guarantees that those who are socially and psychologically successful—those who play well with others—will have better reproductive outcomes. So, the genes that determine who we are biologically are subject to social and psychological selection pressures. And that means that even to understand our biology, we must understand our social context.

We thus see that to grant the supervenience of the social and psychological on the biological is not to claim that the biological level has any privileged explanatory role, still less that we can dispense with "higher" levels of analysis in favor of more "fundamental" levels. We can only understand persons if we take a multidimensional perspective that takes all of these levels of description and their complex interactions into account. One way to put this is to say that we are biologically determined to create social structures that provide the context in which we develop psychologically. Our psychology in turn helps to elaborate these social structures, which in turn shape our psychology. This complex psychological and social environment in turn helps to determine our biological heritage as well as its expression in concrete situations. Persons emerge from this looping, spiraling interaction between variables at each of these levels of description. None can be ignored if we want to understand who we are. Let us now turn to some of the specific ways that we emerge as persons.

Becoming Persons

We are born helpless, in need of care, and we are biologically endowed with the resources to seek, to stimulate, and to accept that care. This is a commonplace. But the impact on how we emerge as persons is profound. It means that we come to understand ourselves as persons, and to manifest that personhood not through an immediate first-person awareness of ourselves, as one might expect were we selves, but rather through our awareness of and our recognition by second persons. The contemporary British developmental psychologist Vasudevi Reddy has explored this aspect of our cognitive and affective development in great depth.[9] Her empirical work and her reflection on that work provide compelling evidence regarding how early human infants recognize second persons, and how central that recognition is not only to their later recognition of third persons, but, more importantly, to their own self-conception as first persons.[10]

Reddy asks, "what does it take to be aware that someone is attending to you?"[11] This apparently simple question raises two others that are essential to understanding how we come to be persons: First, what does it take to recognize another's attention? Second, what does it take to recognize oneself as the object of that attention? Reddy begins to answer these questions when she says, "the awareness of self as the object of others' attention . . . must lead to, rather than result from, representations of self and other as psychological entities. This perspective assumes what one might call a 'second-person' approach to the developing awareness of self and other."[12] That is, our awareness of ourselves as subjects dawns with our awareness of those who address us and who we address. In other words, the first-person and the second-person are co-emergent. We cannot understand our own self-consciousness without understanding its emergence through our consciousness of others.

Reddy provides evidence for this co-emergence through observation of infant-parent interactions in first two years of life. By age two–four months, infants respond to another's gaze with pleasure or fear, and attempt to engage attention and gaze. By six–eight months, they monitor the gaze of others and orient their own gaze in response. Importantly, this monitoring, she argues, includes affective awareness. As early as two months of age, she shows, infants exhibit coyness, embarrassment, pride, and pleasure and respond to the affective states of those with whom they interact. The affective and the cognitive co-emerge, and do so essentially in these dyadic contexts. In short, the emergence of subjectivity is inextricably bound up with the recognition of another's attention and mood, and so with the primitive awareness of oneself as the object of another subject. The second person is hence inextricably bound up with the first.

Reddy also argues that early dyadic infant-parent interactions involve the spontaneous perception of action as intentional, and that these interactions are often dialogical, and so involve the explicit representation of subjective *difference* between the participants.[13] Infants and caregivers, that is to say, are explicitly exchanging information in these interactions; each is cognizant both of what she has to communicate and of the knowledge and ignorance of the other. This is important because it shows that even before they master language, infants represent the difference in perspective between themselves and those with whom they interact, and the distinct roles each takes in dyadic interactions. The implications of this awareness of difference for the development of personhood are profound.

Infants interact with their caregivers not through language, but through nonlinguistic actions. Those actions, whether playful or protesting, even though they are nonverbal, are *interpreted*. And when we interpret somebody as meaning something, we are on the way to taking them to be a person. A parent reaches for an infant, and the infant prepares her body to be lifted; she interprets the gesture as a reaching for her. A parent plays peekaboo, and the infant interprets the covering and revealing of the face as an enticement to play. The infant makes facial expressions or gestures to attract the attention of the caregiver or to engage him in interaction. The infant is hence immediately attributing intentionality, interest, and subjectivity to the other, taking the second person to be a person capable of experiencing her own actions and with intentions of his own.[14]

This recognition of the difference between oneself and another is very important. It is part of the foundation of our development as persons and our recognition of ourselves and of others as occupants of roles. For these interactions are not only *dyadic*; they are *dialogical*, with each participant taking a different role. The infant recognizes the difference in perspective, in intention, and in capacity of the second person. Subjectivity is hence understood, from the beginning of human life, not as uniform, but as varying from person to person; the infant's own subjective states, intentions, and experiences are not simply projected onto the dialogical partner; they are *differentiated* from them. That is, early in life, infants come to understand that minds constitute a multiplicity, with many different instances.[15]

Reddy draws these insights together into a comprehensive account of the origins of social cognition in the second-person perspective. She writes:

> The typical development of social cognition . . . originates in . . . second-person engagements that irresistibly involve the infant, changing not only the infant cognizer's capacity to cognize, but also that which develops to be cognized. The emotional involvement of persons, in particular those most salient of emotional involvements that occur in second-person engagements where the infant is directly addressed or responded to by another, becomes the crucible of cognition.[16]

But if cognition and affective maturation begin in early-childhood second-person interaction, the second person does not lose importance once one becomes explicitly aware of third persons and of oneself as part of a community of second and third persons. Second persons remain important, Reddy emphasizes, through adulthood. She continues:

> Both types of experiences, second-person involvements and third-person observations, must influence each other and both may be necessary even for stable pre-inferential perceptions of other minds. . . . But being addressed as a You and addressing the other as a You arouses emotional responses differently from watching someone else being addressed, and engenders—even if briefly—a mutuality and suspension of separateness. The other becomes a person to you, someone who knocks you off balance or enters your consciousness in a more fundamental way than when you are largely untouched by the other, or just watching them.[17]

We respond in special ways—with distinct neural signatures—to being addressed by our names, or even as "you," and our affective arousal is higher when in dyadic interactions than when observing others.[18] We not only become who we are in early second-person interactions, but we manifest who we are in these interactions in maturity.[19]

This engagement requires a complex co-constituted intentional situation: first, we must be open to engage with others. To be open in this sense is to see others as persons, as subjects in their own right. We do not address trees or tables as *You*, only persons, and address presupposes the possibility of uptake. But this is not enough: to address another as a second person presupposes that the adressor recognizes the addressee as a person. Just as I do not address them, I do not take myself to be addressed by the sound of the surf or thunder, or by birds. Address requires that I find myself in a dyad not only in which I recognize the other's personhood, but in which I am also respected by the other as a person.[20]

But there is a higher-level requirement as well. If I am truly to address you, whether as an infant or as an adult, I have to be able to recognize the fact that you recognize me. And I must suppose that we each recognize this reciprocity. If I do not recognize this complex relationship, then even if you might take me to be addressing you, I cannot take myself to be doing so. Second-person recognition, even in infancy, is hence an act of higher-order cognition in which I take you to take me as someone whose messages are worthy of uptake. But at the same time, to do so is to see myself as just such a being. All of this shows that first-person awareness of ourselves as subjects is hence possible in the context of second-person relations. This context constitutes the two-way street on which we members of species *Homo sapiens* can come to lead lives as persons.

This developmental story is important because it demonstrates just how co-constituted our subjectivity is. We may take ourselves naïvely to be independent subjects who accidentally discover others; we may take our access to our own minds to be more fundamental than our access to others; we may take association to be somehow accidental or optional. But in each case we are wrong to do so. We become persons through our interactions with other persons; and as persons, we fully manifest who we are only in such interactions.

The fact that as persons we lack independent selves—and that our personhood is brought into existence as we learn our roles in interaction with others—hence does not reduce us to nonexistence, but rather explains how beings like us can come to be in the first place. To regard ourselves as selfless persons is not to denigrate but to make sense of our reality, and to recognize that our lives are only possible and can only have meaning in the context of a world. We turn in the next chapter to a discussion of how it is that we construct lives as persons and find those lives meaningful in the absence of any self.

9

Being in the World

LIVING AS A PERSON

Bees and Hives

Human beings, although so like other animals in some respects, are unusual in the animal kingdom in other very important respects. One of those respects, of course, is our use of language. Language is a signaling system that fulfills some of the purposes served by other animal communication systems. But, because of its recursivity, flexibility, and expressive power, language comes to reshape our cognition and to enable our complex societies, a point to which we will return shortly. Human language is made possible by three distinct conditions, each of which is important in constituting us as persons.

First, we require the neurobiological adaptations that subserve language acquisition and use. We are biologically wired for language, and without this wiring it would be impossible for us to learn or to use it. Second, we have been selected in our evolution because of the success that language confers in the human social niche. That is, we have evolved to use language, and by using language, we have created a linguistic niche that ensures that selection pressure will prefer those who are linguistically competent: niche is as important as biology in determining what kinds of creatures we become.

Finally, we must have a propensity to recognize and to be governed by systems of conventional norms. That is, we must be tuned not only to notice and to conform to regularities in the behavior of those among whom we live, but also to take those regularities to constitute norms that bind us. We must, in other words, take conformity to those regularities to be obligatory. This suggests that we have evolved to recognize and to respect norms of various kinds, and we have thereby created a *social* niche that in turn reinforces that evolutionary pressure. These are among the most important social structures responsible for enabling the social roles that constitute us as persons.

Linguistic rules and conventions are what make meaning possible.[1] Words are meaningful only because there are rules governing their use. These rules constitute the distinction between correct and incorrect usage that underlies meaning. But there are countless other conventions or customs that acquire normative force through establishing patterns of behavior so central to our lives that we live those lives only through the confidence that we have in the regularity of those patterns. Think for instance of the custom of driving on a particular side of the road, or of stopping for a red light. Customs of greeting, of making and keeping promises, of paying for what we purchase also structure our lives. There are countless more. Human beings seem to have evolved to seek, to detect, and then to rely on regularities in one another's behavior.

Once again, this biological and psychological feature leads us to structure our social lives and our cultures around networks of customs. Those cultures then create niches in which the ability to detect and the tendency to respect custom are selected. All of this generates a virtuous spiral, a spiral that produces our highly regulated lives and social orders. This regulation, paradoxically, is what makes it possible for us to be the creative individuals we are, for creativity requires meaning, mutual recognition, and forms of life in which it makes sense to be creative.

David Hume referred to this as "the concealed influence of custom."[2] Before Hume, English legal theorists such as John Fortescue (1670–1746) and Edmund Burke (1729–1787) had argued that habitual patterns of behavior naturally become social customs; that social customs naturally lead participants in the societies in which they arise to expect conformity to them; and that these expectations of conformity naturally become norms, which in turn are codified in laws. To say that we are creatures of custom is thus not simply to note our propensity for regularity or mutual imitation; it is to identify one of the deepest aspects of our nature, one that allows us to be social and hence that enables us to develop the qualities we cultivate in early parent-child interactions into those that constitute us as adult persons. That is the propensity not only to *imitate*, but to take behavioral convergence to be *normative*.[3]

If we turn from a Scottish to an Indian Buddhist context, we also find an account of persons as conventional or *lokavyāvahāra* entities—entities that only exist in the context of everyday interactions. This account was, as we have seen, developed by Buddhist philosophers as a critique of the view that a human being is, or possesses, an independently existent self or *ātman*. To say that we are socially constructed is—according to this tradition—not just to say that some superficial properties, such as our social status or occupations, are constructed socially, or that some of our preferences and habits reflect our cultures. All of that is true, but Buddhist philosophers think that it only scratches the surface. Convention, or custom, constitutes our own identity and the nature of the world we inhabit.

We can spell this idea out in the terms of Vasudevi Reddy's idea that to be a person is to be an addressor and an addressee, and that is to be one who takes oneself and others to be interlocutors, a status that is only achievable, and only comprehensible, in a social context. If we take this aspect of personhood as seriously as I have been arguing that we must, it follows that our very being, like the institutions in the context of which we function, is socially constructed: we are essentially social animals, or, as Bernard Mandeville (1670–1733) would have it, complicated bees.

One does not come to understand a beehive by studying individual bees and scaling up; instead, one understands an individual bee by understanding how a hive works, and what that bee's role is therein. You don't first observe a lot of theatrical roles and then put them all together to figure out what the theatre is; instead, you understand a theatrical role by first knowing about the theatre. The same is true regarding our understanding of persons: one does not come to understand our cultures by understanding how an individual *Homo sapiens* organism works, and then scaling up; one understands how a person works by understanding our cultures and our multiple roles therein. And there is no place for a *self* in the story that these analogies suggest. We are too bound up with others for that. This means that in order to understand who we are, and what our lives are, we must take the social level of analysis at least as seriously as we do the psychological and the biological.

Adult Subjectivity and Personhood

We saw in the previous chapter how our subjectivity develops in second-person interactions, and that we can only know ourselves as subjects to the extent that others address us (and that we address others) in the context of a mutual expectation of understanding. As we acquire language, we come to address one another in that medium, and our self-understanding as well as our understanding of others is permeated by the metaphor of linguistic meaning. When we ascribe others' beliefs, desires, intentions, hopes, and fears, we do so by ascribing content to their mental states that we express in sentences. We believe *that grass is green,* desire *that our party wins the election,* fear *that they won't,* etc.

When we ascribe contentful mental states to others— something we do constantly—we neither observe nor hypothesize that there are little sentences in their brains. That would be impossible. There are no such little sentences inscribed in neural matter, and even if there were, we could never see them. Instead, we engage in an act of interpretation, using sentences and the meaningfulness of language as a model by means of which to understand human behavior and cognition, a way of making sense of what we and others do. Thus, language is one more metaphor that mediates our understanding of one another.

It is less obvious—but no less true—that we do the same when we come to understand ourselves. We describe our own beliefs, intentions, and so forth in linguistic terms as well, and we do so without observing or positing inner sentences. This is the only way that we *can* understand ourselves, in a constant act of auto-interpretation.[4] Once language is in the picture, any pre-linguistic innocence that guides our interactions is lost forever. For this is the moment when we become fully responsible to a norm-constituting community in order to make and to absorb meaning.

When we join the community of language users, we tacitly agree to follow the rules for usage of linguistic terms that are enforced by our community. When we learn to reason, we learn to conform to the rules of reasoning respected in our community. When we learn to claim knowledge, we learn to conform to the epistemic norms of our community. When we use language as a model for thought, we import all of these commitments to our understanding of one another and of ourselves. To regard ourselves or others as thinkers is hence to regard ourselves and others as members of a community that constitutes and that is constituted by norms.

We should remember that the word *I* is first and foremost a linguistic item. So, when I use the first-person pronoun, I undertake certain commitments, the kinds of commitments essential to participation in a linguistic community. These commitments depend both on the fact that to speak is always to address another, and on the fact that to speak is to agree to use the words I utter in conformity with the grammatical and semantic rules that govern my language. In particular, to use *I* is to take my addressees to be capable of being addressed as *you*, to be persons who can also use *I* to express their own subjectivity, who can understand what I say, and who can address me as *you*. It is also to regard others as *he, she,* or *they*—that is, to recognize a broad linguistic and social community that institutes and enforces the norms that make speech and address possible.

In short, the possibility of speech—and hence of adult subjectivity, since we understand the contents of our own minds in terms of categories derived from speech—depends on *intersubjectivity*. And this, to repeat, is simply because speech presupposes both addressees who can be expected themselves to be subjects and a context of meaning-constituted conventions instituted by others whose subjectivity we also presume. So, even our own self-knowledge, and, therefore, also adult human subjectivity in which we recognize ourselves as persons, are essentially intersubjective phenomena, not private.[5] To be a person truly is to be an ensemble player, not a soloist, in more senses than one.

Any account of how we know ourselves and others according to which we first encounter ourselves, then our immediate interlocutors, and then others, building our understanding of others by analogy to that we have of ourselves—as we would if we were selves instead of persons—is hence incoherent. Instead, we come in infancy to understand ourselves and our interlocutors together. This understanding becomes articulate and reflective through the mediation of language and a raft of other social conventions. And this mediation is possible only in the context of a seamless understanding both of the community in which we participate, and of our mutual relations to one another in that community—relations that constitute the normativity that makes understanding possible.

This takes us to another aspect of personhood, and another that distinguishes it from selfhood: to perceive someone as a person—whether myself, my partner, or a stranger—is to see them as *making sense*, as having *meaningful* thoughts, and as saying things that have meaning. But to take something to make sense, and so to take someone to have a cognitive or an affective life, to play a social role, is always an interpretative act, whether that interpretation is explicit or implicit.[6]

The sapience in adult *Homo sapiens* therefore always arises through our mutual interpretation, so is always beholden to norms, and so is always *collective*. In taking myself to be a person, I take you to be a person; in taking you to be a person, I take them to be persons; that is, I take all of us to be committed and responsible to norms of reasonable interpretation. I also take us all to be collectively committed to the constitution of a rule-governed linguistic community in the context of which meaning can be constituted, and so in which fully articulate address is possible.

This all means that we create ourselves and one another as persons in the context of our social interactions, social interactions that constitute the structures and institutions that allow us to live lives that make sense, and that allow us to make sense of our lives. And these interactions themselves are only possible between persons who constitute, are bound by, and are constituted by being bound by the norms those interactions institute.

This is not as circular as it sounds. Think of it more as one more instance of the spiral we encountered earlier, grounded in our predisposition as social apes to recognize one another and to recognize ourselves in others' eyes, as well as our predisposition to learn language and to be sensitive to and to conform to the behavioral regularities we observe around us. These predispositions enable and encourage us gradually to enter into the linguistic and social practices of our communities and to recognize others and ourselves as persons, playing our respective roles in a common social space. The social space we thereby collaborate in constructing in turn shapes all of us. It is also instrumental in selecting for individuals who will thrive in that space, creating this social, behavioral, and evolutionary spiral.

Participation in this spiral, as I have been emphasizing, is natural to us. We have evolved for just such a life, a life in which we create customs, and in which custom creates us. And as Hume notes, that influence of custom is often "concealed." That is, we participate in customs of which we may be only dimly, or tacitly, aware, but which nonetheless shape us, such as those that determine the grammar of our languages and the meanings of the words we use, as well as other subtle social regularities to which we become attuned.

Other customs, such as those that govern driving, some aspects of etiquette, or political behavior, might require our more explicit awareness and endorsement. But even so, we might note two important qualifications: First, the very ability to become aware of such customs and the tendency to conform to them itself rests on psychological dispositions of which we may be unaware, as well as the pervasive influence of language. Second, even those conventions into which we enter voluntarily shape us in ways of which we might be unaware. Politics, etiquette, sport, and the other institutions in which we participate shape our thought, our values, and in turn give rise to yet another niche in which we as a species evolve.

We are hence constructed as persons both by our intentional, conscious participation in social structures and by our tacit participation in them; that construction includes both attitudes and roles of which we are explicitly aware and those that may be merely implicit. To be shaped by and to shape this spiral requires us to be in constant open causal interaction with our physical and social environment; it requires that our behavior and thought are conditioned by that environment. This is the flexibility and the embeddedness of persons, not the isolation and constancy of selves. Indeed, there is no place for the self—for the serpent in the wall—in this story. At best it would be a fifth wheel; in fact, as I have argued, it is an incoherent posit.

This all brings us back to what is right about Evan Thompson's suggestion that we have "narrative selves," a suggestion we considered and rejected in chapter 6. We can now see more clearly why the idea that narrative is central to our identity is correct, and why the idea that it constructs a *self* is wrong. Among our central social practices, practices we learn early on and in which we engage throughout our lives are storytelling and narrative explanation. We tell stories in conversation, at bedtime, in the high art of the novel or the opera, when we introduce ourselves, when we describe others, and on and on. For most of us, it would be hard to identify a day in which we did not tell someone—if only ourselves—at least a brief story.

And we use those stories to make sense of our behavior and attitudes in specific circumstances and to make sense of the biographical arcs of our lives. We explain our decision to take a bus rather than to drive a car by talking about how our commitment to the environment structures our life, or our decision to vote for this candidate rather than that one by how her candidacy enhances the life we lead. In eulogies we strive to present the life of the departed as a coherent whole. Narrative is perhaps the most important vehicle for achieving self-understanding. Philosophers such as Friedrich Nietzsche (1844–1900), as well as the contemporary scholars Daniel Hutto and Evan Thompson, get this exactly right.[7]

But there is a dark side to narrative as well. For one thing, as we saw in chapter 3, we are not the sole authors of the stories in which we participate, and some of these tales may be deeply destructive. For another, it is all too easy to take the characters in the narratives we coauthor to exist independently of the stories. And just as we shouldn't ever think that Hamlet has any reality outside of the play, we shouldn't ever think that we as persons have any reality outside of the narratives in which we participate. In one sense, we are as fictional as Shakespeare's creations: we are constituted as characters through the telling of a story; we are absolutely real within the bounds of that story; we are created, not discovered; and we have no reality at all outside of the context of the stories in which we figure. This is why we are *persons*, and not *selves*.

But we are *real* persons, and not *imaginary* persons. Therefore, in another sense, we are different from Hamlet and his

cohort, and that difference is every bit as important as the simi-
larity. Shakespeare's fiction is local, optional, and its roles need
not be instantiated; the fiction in which we play our parts is
global and mandatory. And the roles we play are necessarily
instantiated by biologically real creatures. We, unlike literary persons, are *embodied, embedded,* and *enactive* in our world. All three
of these differences are important. Let us take them in turn.

We begin with the distinction between the local and the
global. Plays, novels, short stories, and fairy tales, unlike news
reports, biographies, and histories, create characters and their
contexts that are independent eddies within the larger current
of life. While these characters and contexts hang together internally, they are dissociated from, and often inconsistent with,
the characters and contexts we share in ordinary life. They
don't have birth certificates. Nobody outside of these stories
interacts physically with them. They have no direct impact on
history, however much indirect impact they may have through
our reading.

Those of us who figure in our own grand social narrative,
however, are connected globally to one another and to history.
Our lives have broad and direct effects on countless others. We
leave traces that span reality, and that are not confined between
the covers of a book or to the minds of those who read it. This
globality of the narrative in which we figure is one important
difference between imaginary and real fictional characters:
while it doesn't undermine our fictional status, it is one aspect
of our lives that confers on us the reality that facts enjoy. That
is what it is for us to *enact* our personhood.

We have a choice regarding whether to read *Hamlet,* and a
choice regarding whether to take the story and the characters
Shakespeare offers us seriously. It is an *optional* fiction. We have
no choice, however, regarding whether to take seriously the

story in which we play our parts. To be sure, we are forced to make choices about how the roles we play are articulated, choices that at least partly determine the narrative arcs of our lives and of those with whom we interact. But we are *forced* to make those choices, and we cannot simply opt out of, or ignore, the stories in which we figure as protagonists. As Heidegger puts it, we are *thrown* (*geworfen*) into the worlds we inhabit.

As a consequence of this thrownness, we cannot disregard others any more than we can disregard ourselves; we cannot choose to disbelieve or to set aside the narratives that confer personal identities and roles on us. Even to turn away when our attention is demanded, even to shirk our moral or social responsibilities, is to participate—however unwillingly—in these dramas. To act in bad faith is still to act. All of this is to say that the narratives that constitute us as persons also constitute our world, and so are *mandatory* fictions. This mandatoriness is another aspect of our human life that confers facthood on it, that constitutes its *truth,* however fictional that truth might be. That is what it is for us to be *embedded* in our world.

Finally, we should observe that the characters in literary works remain *abstract* in an important sense. Those roles are played only when they are deliberately staged, and even when they are staged, those who play them do so only for a short time. And that role-playing is itself a sub-part of the roles those actors play as *persons,* even when those are the roles of professional actors. Moreover, these literary roles are independent of anyone who might play them. Hamlet might be performed by Sir Laurence Olivier or by Benedict Cumberbatch. But the role remains the same, and neither Olivier nor Cumberbatch actually becomes a Shakespearean character in playing that role. Our roles as persons, however, are closely tied to specific biological organisms, to particular members of species *Homo sapiens.* We are born to play these roles, and we have only limited choice regarding them. That is what it is for us to be *embodied* and to be *embedded* in the world into which we are thrown, and to *enact* ourselves as persons in that collectively constituted world.

For all of these reasons, we can draw a distinction between what is true and what is false within the domain of the fictional; and that is to distinguish between what we can and must trust, and what we can't take too seriously. We fall on the true side; Hamlet, Ahab, and Bilbo Baggins lie on the false side: however real they may be within the more limited fictions they inhabit, their reality does not leak into the domain in which we enact our personhood. But we cannot infer from that that we have any existence outside of that grand global narrative: we are not independent selves, but interdependent persons.

The "Problem" of Other Minds

These reflections sometimes take us to surprising places. We have been talking about what it is to be a person. To recognize someone as a person is in part to recognize them as someone who can be understood as possessing a mind. And, as we have seen, to understand ourselves as persons is to understand ourselves as members of communities of persons, and therefore to recognize others as persons as well. All of this is rather obvious. But this situation both raises and solves a philosophical problem, generally called "the problem of other minds." It is useful at this point to see both why that problem is sometimes thought to require a solution, and why it never even arises in ordinary life. The problem of other minds bothers a lot of people, and arises in multiple traditions at many times in the history of philosophy. While I believe that it is a pseudo-problem, it can easily grip us. But its grip loosens as we dissolve the self illusion.

In a nutshell, the problem of other minds goes like this: I know immediately that I have a mind, because I am directly and intimately aware of my own inner cognitive and affective life. But when I see others, all I see is their external behavior. How do I know that they are not automata, simulations of persons, with no inner mental states or minds at all? I can't know this by perception, since minds are not perceptible. And I can't know it by inference, since everything I observe is consistent with the automaton hypothesis. I can't even know it by induction, since the only case I have is my own, and by hypothesis, I may be very different from others, and so cannot infer from my own case, leaving aside the fact that it is but a single case. So, how do I know that anyone else has a mind? This is the problem. I hope that you can feel its grip.

As Wittgenstein saw in his *Philosophical Investigations*, the problem of other minds so posed is a double problem, concerning both our knowledge of other minds and the very meaning of the vocabulary we use to talk about minds. The first aspect of the problem is that, as we just saw, we have neither perceptual nor inferential knowledge of the minds of others, and no good inductive reasons for thinking that others have minds at all. The second aspect of the problem is deeper: if we can never *know* whether our attribution of inner states to others is true or false—not because the evidence happens to be hard to get, but because nothing would even *count* as evidence—we literally could have no idea what it would be for these attributions to be true or false. To put this another way, if our only concept of a mind is that of our own mind, to say that others have minds would be to say that they have our minds, which makes no sense whatsoever.

But here is the real sting in this problem: if we don't know what we mean when we attribute psychological states to others, we don't know what we mean when we attribute them to ourselves, either. This is because the very problem arises regarding how we can understand others to be *like us, in having minds,* which is the problem of what it is to have a mind in the first place. If we don't know what their minds are, we don't know what ours are, either. This is troubling, suggesting an intolerably deep self-alienation.

It is important to feel this perplexity, so as to diagnose it and get rid of it once and for all, and this perplexity is deeply connected to the topic at hand. We can now see that the problem of other minds arises from thinking of ourselves and of others as *selves,* as isolated, independent loci of subjectivity, with our subjective worlds located in interior spaces immediately available to us, and impenetrable to others. Only if we start by thinking of minds this way can we get the problem going, for only then are our minds available immediately to us, and those of others opaque. And, as we have seen, thinking about minds and about ourselves, this way is almost irresistible. It is the irresistibility of that self illusion that makes the problem of other minds so irresistible as well, since they stand and fall together. But now that we have learned to resist the temptation of the self illusion, we can dissolve the problem of other minds once and for all.

The apparent problem arises from what looks like a vast difference between our knowledge of our own psychological states and those of others. If our own mental states are immediately available to us, but those of others are invisible, there is no possibility of understanding mental state ascription, or knowing the minds of others. But, as we have seen, this impossibility has a nasty consequence: there would also be no possibility of knowing our own inner states.

This is because to know our own states is to know them as *instances* of *kinds* of states, as pains, longings, or beliefs that

Ulan Bator is the capital of Mongolia. If I do not know that my belief is a belief, or do not know what its content is, I don't really know it. But we can only know *kinds* if we know them to have multiple instances. To know that this rose is red requires me to be able to recognize multiple roses and to know what it is not only for this rose to be red, but also for a fire engine to be red.

The same goes for minds and mental states. To recognize anything as a mind is to recognize it as one of a class of things, and to recognize something as a belief that Ulan Bator is the capital of Mongolia is to recognize it as an instance of states of that kind. This goes for my mind and mental states as much as it does for the minds and mental states of others. So, I cannot know my own mind without knowing that there are others, and I cannot know my own mental states without knowing them as instances of mental states that others entertain as well.

And here lies the key to the solution of the problem of other minds: the fundamental premise that generates the problem is the supposition that psychological concepts don't have that kind of generality. That is, the problem of other minds rests on the assumption that I know my own mind and mental states *not* as instances of kinds, but *directly*. It also presupposes that I can't know the minds and states of others in the same way. And once we make that move, given their apparent interiority, it follows that we cannot know them in any other way.

When we take the second-person perspective seriously, though, our status as persons instead of as selves provides the clue to the way out of this particular fly bottle. The problem of other minds gets going by inviting us to think of our psychological states as existing independent of our interpretation and context, like pebbles on the beach of our consciousness to be discovered and examined, and as lying in our interior, while everything else is exterior. If we think that each of us has a private inner beach, and that each of us knows our inner lives just by examination of independently existing facts, we are stuck. But when we take seriously the fact that we are always interpreting one another, and even interpreting ourselves, that we are characters whose psychology we and others author together, the gulf between ourselves and others vanishes along with the metaphor of the inner private world. For on this model, our understanding of our own minds and of those of others arises not from the discovery of primordial facts, but instead from acts of interpretation.

It follows from the interpretative character of this knowledge that, like all acts of interpretation, our judgments about the contents of minds—whether our own or someone else's—are answerable only to the standards of cogency and good sense that we use to evaluate good readings of a text, or interpretations of a work of art. We do not ask whether these judgments correspond to a preexisting reality the nature of which is independent of interpretation. The important point is that this goes both for self-understanding and for the understanding of others. The same conceptual categories and the same acts of interpretation that give us knowledge of our own minds give us knowledge of those of others, and without knowing those others, we could not even know ourselves.[8]

To treat our understanding of ourselves and others in terms of interpretation is not to deny that there is any truth of the matter regarding what we think and how we feel, to assert that anything goes. This is because interpretation does not reflect, so much as *constitute*, the reality of our cognitive lives. Any interpretation, whether of *Hamlet* or of my mind, stands or falls on the grounds of its harmony with all of our other interpretations. And that harmony is sufficient to constitute truth; its absence is sufficient for falsehood. That is, while the entire ensemble of social and interpretative conventions in which we participate may *constitute the context* in which it is true that I believe that Ulan Bator is the capital of Mongolia, once that context is in place, there is a clear fact of the matter regarding whether or not I hold this belief.

This is no different from how we already understand most of our norm-constituted institutions. As we saw earlier, nobody believes that we just discover money; we create it. And we do so by interpreting various bits of paper, metal, and states of computing machinery as having monetary value. In virtue of that interpretation, those values become real. Money, that is, gets its very existence as well as its value through our collective acts of interpretation, not through any preexisting reality on which we stumbled. It is fictional.

But this does not mean that there is no truth of the matter regarding whether a particular piece of paper is a dollar note, or what my bank balance is. There is fact within that fiction; the creation of the fiction, and its globality, mandatoriness, and use constitute its truth. And the fact that in the United States we simply decided to drive on the right does not make it any less a *fact* that that is the correct side on which to drive; instead, that is what makes it a fact in the first place. That is, while the whole system is created, once created it in turn creates a context in which particular statements can be true or false in virtue of the interpretations already assigned to others. That is how it is with us, when considered not as hominids, but as persons.

"But wait," you might protest, "maybe this goes for mental states like beliefs, but there is still a problem about what it feels like to be me, about sensory experience. Even if I might know that others can *think,* how can I know that they *feel* anything? Maybe their lights are on, but nobody's home! I at least know that I feel as well as think. So, the problem of other minds hasn't really been solved." This is a powerful intuition, and it is closely related to Zahavi's idea that our own experience has *for-me-ness*. It is part and parcel of the supposition that we are selves. The reply is therefore also closely related to our reply to that idea in chapter 5.

The idea that I might have an inner life while others don't raises the possibility of what contemporary philosophers such as David Chalmers call *zombies*.[9] A zombie in this sense is a being that is exactly like us cognitively and behaviorally, but that lacks any inner life or real sensory experience. To worry that I alone have such an inner life is to suppose that others might be zombies. We will now see why that makes no sense, and so that the supposition that others may have no inner life, despite being like me in all other respects, makes no sense either.

Suppose that there are zombies. Since, in order for this version of the problem of other minds to make any sense, these zombies must be just like us in all respects except for their inner life, they share with us the conviction that they have inner lives, including sensory experience. On this supposition, however, they are wrong. But how could they be? Imagine arguing with someone who sincerely believes that she has sensory experience and trying to convince her that she does not! Better yet, ask yourself, "Are you a zombie?" You will probably reply that you know that you are not. But notice that you can't know that, since if you were a zombie, you would believe that you have an inner life just as you do now. There is no way you could tell! So, if zombies were possible, we could never know that we are not zombies. And in that case, we could not know that we have experience. But that is insane, and self-defeating, since it was our conviction in our knowledge of our own experience that drives this very intuition. It follows that this version of the problem of other minds makes no sense either.

For these reasons, there can be no "problem of other minds" any more than there can be a "problem of other dollars." To be a mind is not to house hidden inner particulars that have their character independent of how we understand them, and that we somehow discover; it is to interpret and to be interpreted; to address and to be addressed; to participate in the complex human conversation, and to share a world with others like us. So, to know that others have minds is not to know that they have mysterious inner worlds, and to know that we have minds is to know that we are like others. We each know immediately that we are minds not through introspection, but through participation. We know that others are minds not through inference and not through clairvoyance, but through co-participation.

To allow ourselves to be addressed by, or to address, another is to take her to be a person, to have a mind; it is at the same time to take ourselves to be persons. This phenomenon of address requires neither reflexive self-consciousness, nor qualitative experience, nor interiority, nor autonomy, nor any of the other properties associated with selves. It only requires us to recognize each other as members of the same community, sharing the same world. But what is it to recognize ourselves and others to be members of a community of persons? It is, we shall see, to see one another as *valuable,* as objects of care and respect. And the deepest reason to forego the myth of the self for the recognition of the reality of the person is that it is persons, not selves, that merit respect and care. We will close our investigation by considering this issue.

Persons and Values

All of this allows us a new perspective on the big questions: What really matters? Why do we value one another? Why do we and our fellows merit respect, rights, consideration, and kindness? That is another way of asking the question, "What is special about people?" And this question leads to another: "When we want to assign value to nonhuman entities, like corporations, organizations, nonhuman animals, ecosystems, or rivers, what kind of status do we give them?" Answering these questions reminds us of just how important personhood is, and shows how irrelevant selves are to our moral and political life.

We care about one another, take one another's desires and welfares seriously, respect one another's rights, and treat one another with consideration—in short, we value one another—to the degree that we embrace one another in a moral and social community. That is, moral valuation depends on seeing one another as *together* in a shared world. This does not require that we agree about everything, or that our projects are the same. We can respect and honor those with whom we share little in the way of beliefs, values, or way of life. But this kind of moral respect and recognition does require that we see one another as potential fellows in a larger sense: as playing analogous roles in the human world, and so as potential addressees or addressors—more simply, as conversation partners.[10] And conversation requires both a broadly shared background of concerns and presuppositions, and distinct vantage points or perspectives discernible against that shared background.[11] As we have seen, it also presupposes that each party takes the other as one who can take seriously what the other says, and who has something to tell the other.

Our ability to care about others, including distant others we have never met, arises from our ability to see others as sharing in this grand project. For if the project in which we see ourselves as agents—the project of life—is sufficient to give meaning to our own lives, it is also sufficient to give meaning to those others who join us in that project. Just as Hamlet gains his significance in *Hamlet*, so too, do Rosencrantz and Guildenstern, and they matter to one another precisely because they are part of the same drama.

When we recognize each other in this sense—a kind of recognition absolutely fundamental to our collective lives—we recognize our *interdependence*, not our *independence*; our roles and commitments, not our subjectivity; our participation in a shared world, not our spectatorship of a world of which we are independent. In short, this kind of moral and political recognition is the recognition of *persons*, not of *selves*. And this is why it makes sense to think of organizations or natural phenomena as persons, as grounds for treating them with respect, or as grounds for the conferral of rights, even though it would make no sense whatsoever to assert that they have *selves*, even if we thought that we do.

Śāntideva makes this point eloquently in *How to Lead an Awakened Life*. He argues that we can only cultivate attitudes of friendliness and care for others when we are able to project ourselves imaginatively into their situations, when we can regard others as our mothers, when we recognize our thoroughgoing interdependence with them, and when we abandon the fantasy that we and they are the agents of independent, free action. When we do so, he argues, we come to see that suffering is bad not because it is *ours*, but because it is bad, *per se*, no matter whose it is, and that happiness is good not just when it is ours, but wherever it arises.[12]

This attitude of universal care is the foundation of genuine moral concern. When we adopt this attitude, we do not see ourselves and others as isolated, independent selves who happen to find one another in proximity in a featureless abstract landscape, and then have to figure out whether and how to relate to one another. Instead, we see one another as persons who share a world pregnant with meaning—meaning that we collectively create, and which in turn shapes our lives. In seeing one another in this way, we come to appreciate the way we co-constitute one another, and the ways in which we are responsive and responsible to one another.

Selves could never facilitate our moral or collective lives; they could only get in the way. That is why Dōgen writes that "To study the self is to forget the self; to forget the self is to cast off body and mind; to cast off body and mind is to be affirmed by all things." This affirmation is, and can only be, the affirmation of our shared personhood.

10

Getting Over Yourself

DRAWING THIS ALL TOGETHER

IT IS NOW TIME to draw this all together. We have identified Candrakīrti's serpent, and we have shown why we need not fear it. There is no snake in the wall; there is no self at our core. To believe that we have selves is to succumb to a natural illusion, just as we succumb naturally to optical illusions. We are neither substantial subjects who take the world as object, nor free actors who intervene in an otherwise law-governed natural world. Instead, we are persons: hyper-social organisms embedded in the world, in open causal interaction with our environments and with each other; complex causal continua who play complex social roles.

We have seen that while there is a powerful psychological drive to reification that results in the self illusion, and while that drive has been sublimated into sophisticated accounts of that self and arguments for its reality, we can resist the pull both of that drive and of those arguments. Even the best of those arguments establish only our reality as persons, not as selves, and everything that we might have thought could only be accomplished by a self can be handled just fine by persons.

But we have established more than that. One might have thought that the discovery that we have no self, no *ātman*, no *psyche*, would be the discovery that we are somehow less than we thought we were, that we are diminished in dignity, in freedom, in moral worth, or that our lives are less worthwhile than they would be were we selves. But we have seen that this is wrong. Just as our homes are safer with no snakes hiding in the walls, our lives are better for the fact that we are selfless persons than they could ever have been were we selves. That is, the self you might have thought you were would only get in the way of leading a flourishing life; thinking that you have a self does not enhance but instead impoverishes your life.

This is true, we have seen, for several reasons. First, the kind of self-consciousness that arises from thinking of ourselves as selves gets in the way of fluid expert performance. And even though we might not all be virtuoso pianists, or virtuoso tennis players, we are each capable of being virtuoso friends, virtuoso parents, virtuoso colleagues, or virtuoso citizens, persons who play our respective roles well. We do better at these things when we give up our self illusion than when we focus on that self. Giving up the self, that is, facilitates spontaneity.

Second, to the extent that I think of myself and others as selves, I undermine my ethical life and my ethical engagement with others. The self illusion distorts our own sense of agency, and distorts our attribution of agency to others. It leads us to see ourselves and others as free actors instead of embedded agents, leading to reactive attitudes that fail to reflect reality, and that do nobody any good. To see ourselves as interacting persons allows us to consider the causes and reasons for our own behavior and attitudes, as well as those of others, and encourages us to resolve problems rather than to recriminate, to ameliorate situations rather than to punish, and to cultivate attitudes that make everyone more effective and happy.

Finally, to see ourselves as persons rather than as selves allows us a richer, more nuanced understanding of who we are, of how we become who we are, and of the importance of our development and social context to our identity. We are not isolated individuals who happen to choose to live together; we are social animals who only become the individuals we do in social contexts that scaffold our flourishing. We can only make sense of our lives and see them as meaningful when we understand our personhood and when we give up the fantasy of independence encoded in the idea of a self.

When people first hear about the idea of selflessness, they often find it disturbing. They think that this is the nihilistic idea that we don't really exist. But that only makes sense if you think that to exist is to be a self. Once we see that the self is illusory, we see that that can't be right. The fact that a dollar is not a piece of paper does not mean that dollars don't exist, and the fact that we are not selves doesn't mean that we do not exist. Instead, for beings like us, to exist is to be a person—a socially constituted being embedded in a rich and meaningful world—just as for things like dollars, to exist is to be a unit of currency embedded in an economic system. To deny that we are persons would be to deny that we exist. So, the self illusion, although it seems to confer a greater reality on us than would mere conventional personhood, in fact undermines the very reality that makes us who we are. To accept that you have no self is not to reject your identity; it is to reclaim your humanity.

The finer the hair, the more important it is to split it.

—SANDY HUNTINGTON

NOTES

Preface

1. See Beckwith, *Greek Buddha: Pyrrho's Encounter with Buddhism in Central Asia* (2015), McEvilley, *The Shape of Ancient Thought* (2002), and Kuzminski, *Pyrrhonism: How the Ancient Greeks Reinvented Buddhism* (2008) for detailed discussions of these tangled origins. I discuss these ideas in my *"Epochē and Śūnyatā: Skepticism East and West"* (1990) and in *Engaging Buddhism: Why It Matters to Philosophy* (2015).

2. My own discussions are to be found in *Engaging Buddhism: Why It Matters to Philosophy* (2015) and in *The Concealed Influence of Custom: Hume's "Treatise" from the Inside Out* (2019). See Collins (2008) and Siderits (2017) for excellent discussions of Buddhist views of selfless persons.

3. See Strohminger and Nichols, *"The Essential Moral Self"* (2014).

Chapter 1

1. References to Indian texts are by chapter and verse. For good translations of *Introduction to the Middle Way,* see Huntington and Wangchen (1995) or Chandrakīrti and Mipham (2005).

2. The Tibetan philosopher Tsongkhapa (1357–1419) refers to this as *identification of the object of negation,* and he argues that this must be the starting point of any critical philosophical analysis.

3. A good English translation of the Upaniṣads is Olivelle (2008).

4. A good English translation of the *Bhagavad Gītā* is Stoler Miller (1986).

5. Martin Heidegger (1889–1976) was a German existential phenomenologist. In his magnum opus *Being and Time* (original 1927; English translation 1996) he argues that we construct our own identities through our commitments and activities in the world, a world of entities and persons constituted by the interplay of the commitments and activities of the persons with whom we share it.

6. Owen Flanagan, in *The Problem of the Soul* (2002), also regiments the language in this way. His account of the distinction, his critique of the idea of the self, and his

defense of the reality of persons are very much in harmony with my own. See especially his discussion in chapters 5 and 6.

7. Ganeri (2017) agrees that this model of the self as the author of experience and the agent of action is the target of Buddhist analyses. He proposes, drawing on the Theravāda Buddhist tradition, that we think not of a *self* as that which mediates our experiential and agential interaction with the world, but rather as *attention*. See also Ganeri (2012, chapter 1) for a nice account of the self as a *place* for experience, and an extensive investigation into the variety of positions one can distinguish regarding the self. Ganeri argues that the Buddhist and Humean view that I am defending is an instance of a *no-place* theory.

8. See R. Thurman's *Tsongkhapa's Speech of Gold in "The Essence of True Eloquence"* (2014), pp. 243–45.

9. It is interesting to see that Hume makes a similar point with regard to the equally instinctive and equally incoherent belief that we are in immediate sensory contact with the external world: this view can't be the product of philosophy, even though a rich set of philosophical arguments have been inspired by it and attempt to vindicate it. [*Treatise* 1.4.2] All citations to the *Treatise* reference book, part, and section (and paragraph, when material is quoted). So, this one denotes book 1, part 4, section 2.

10. See especially chapters 1 and 2. This idea is taken up in a different register by the twentieth-century sociologist Ernest Becker (1997) as part of his theory of terror management. One important difference between their views is that while Śantideva takes this fear to be innate, Becker emphasizes its social dimensions. There are several excellent translations of *How to Lead an Awakened Life*, including Crosby and Skilton (2014), Wallace and Wallace (1997), and Shantideva (2006).

11. See *Treatise* 2.1.2. I discuss this at greater length in Garfield (2019), chapter 3.

Chapter 2

1. For an English translation of *The Questions of King Milinda*, see Horner (1964).

2. One might also ask whether the analogy fails because there is something special about the fact that we, unlike chariots, are *alive*. So, while we can remain alive through a certain amount of degeneration or dismemberment, if we are disassembled—whether violently or through a natural process of aging and death— at some point we, unlike chariots, simply die. It is true that the analogy cannot be pushed too far, and that it won't do as an account of life and death. Nonetheless, it makes the point that is relevant here: that as living persons we cannot be identified either with any particular aspect or part of our being, nor with the collection of them, etc. There is no aspect of our existence properly captured by the idea of a *self*. In

particular, death is not the sudden disappearance of a unique entity with which we were identified when alive.

3. There are delicate questions we might ask about the structure of this continuum, including what we should say about the moment when one flame is being used to light another, when the lamp used to light a second lamp continues to burn for a while as the second lamp starts to burn, or when a single lamp is used to light two different lamps. Questions such as these occasioned some interesting speculation in the Buddhist tradition (Tsongkhapa, *Ocean of Reasoning*, 2006) and in the Western tradition (Parfit, *Reasons and Persons*,1984). But we can leave them aside now. Nāgasena's metaphor is, after all, a metaphor. And all metaphors limp. These details are not directly relevant to the central point: we can ascribe a kind of identity to causally connected sequences in the absence of any underlying substantial continuant.

4. For a more extensive discussion of the *Milindapañha*, see Garfield (2015), pp. 42–54, 106–9. See Collins, *Selfless Persons* (2008), for a very fine philosophical discussion of Theravāda Buddhist accounts of selflessness, and of how these accounts involve the affirmation of the reality of persons.

5. In the Buddhist tradition these are classified into five categories: our bodies, sensations, perceptions, personality traits, and consciousness.

6. Antonio Damasio, in *The Feeling of What Happens* (2000), argues for the existence of a proto-self, an autobiographical self, and a core self. Although this might appear to be at odds with the Buddhist rejection of the self, and with my position that there is no self, it is not. For he regards each of these selves not as a primordial subject, but as a *representation* constructed by a complex set of psychophysical processes, including cognitive, affective, and conative processes, and so he is defending the reality of what we are calling a person. (See, especially, pp. 172–77.) Muhammad Farouque, in *Sculpting the Self* (2021), also might appear to be defending the kind of self that I reject in this study. But he is not. He also uses the word *self* much as I use the word *person*, and defends a view of our identity as complex, constructed, culturally determined, and multidimensional.

7. Richard Sorabji, in *Self: Ancient and Modern Insights about Individuality, Life, and Death* (2006), defends the existence of the self in addition to the person. But he draws this distinction differently, using the word *person* to mean "someone who *has* psychological states and *does* things" (p. 21, emphasis in the original). He uses the word *self*, on the other hand, to indicate the subject who occupies a first-person perspective on their lives, which, he claims, is a "thicker" notion (p. 22). See Sorabji's chapter 16 for his critical discussion of Buddhist refutations of *ātman*, including Candrakīrti's.

8. [1.4.6] When referring to passages in the *Treatise*, it is customary to us this notation, denoting which book, part, and chapter (and even paragraph) to which one is referring, in this case, Book 1, Part 4, Section 6.

9. I address Hume's discussion of the self and his reconstruction of our identity as persons at greater length in chapters 4 and 10 of Garfield (2019).

10. For translations of *Thirty Verses*, see Kochumuttom, *A Buddhist Doctrine of Experience: A New Translation and Interpretation of the Works of Vasubandhu* (2008), Anacker, *Seven Works of Vasubandhu: The Buddhist Psychological Doctor* (2015), or Tzohar, *A Yogācāra Buddhist Theory of Metaphor* (2018). For translations of *Treatise on the Three Natures*, see Kochumuttom (2008), Anacker (2015), or Edelglass and Garfield, *Buddhist Philosophy: Essential Readings* (2009).

11. The commitment to a core being having these four characteristics constitutes the vision of the relation of self to world common to classical Indian Vedānta and to Kantian transcendental idealism.

12. A. C. Mukerji, in *The Nature of Self* (1938), presents a sustained defense of the reality of the self from the standpoint of Vedānta, but in dialogue with much of the Western philosophical tradition (including Kant) and with Buddhist critics of the Vedānta position.

13. See Metzinger, *The Ego Tunnel: The Science of the Mind and the Myth of the Self* (2010), pp. 101–4. For a nice discussion of Uddyotakara on the self, see Ganeri, *The Self: Naturalism, Consciousness, and the First-Person Stance* (2012), chapters 12 and 13, or Chakrabarti, "I Touch What I Saw" (1992), pp. 103–16.

14. Dennett, *Consciousness Explained* (1992).

15. See Chalmers, *The Conscious Mind: In Search of a Fundamental Theory* (1997), or Kriegel, *The Varieties of Consciousness* (2018), for representative defenses of this view.

16. See Thompson, *Mind in Life: Biology, Phenomenology, and the Sciences of Mind* (2010), for a rich articulation of this view, and Westerhoff, *The Non-Existence of the Real World* (2020), for an exploration of the implications of this fact for our understanding of the reality of the external world.

17. For Hume on this topic, see the *Treatise* 2.3.1, and my discussion in *The Concealed Influence of Custom: Hume's "Treatise" from the Inside Out* (2019), pp. 85–89. For Schopenhauer, see his *Essay on the Freedom of the Will* (2005). And see Dennett, *Elbow Room: Varieties of Free Will Worth Wanting* (1984).

18. See A. C. Mukerji's *The Problem of Self* (1938) for an explicit defense of the Vedānta position, and Muhammad Iqbal's *The Reconstruction of Religious Thought in Islam* (2020) for a defense of the same kind of position from the standpoint of Islamic thought, inflected by ideas from F. H. Bradley's *Appearance and Reality* (1893).

19. I address this in greater detail in Garfield (2015), chapter 4.

20. Metzinger carefully explores this illusion in *Being No-One: The Self-Theory Model of Subjectivity* (2004) and *The Ego Tunnel: The Science of the Mind and the Myth of the Self* (2010).

Chapter 3

1. I should note that there is something a bit artificial about the linguistic distinction, since each of these terms has a broad semantic range in English, and in common usage their meanings overlap. But it helps sometimes to stipulate how we are using terms in order to draw clear distinctions, and so I am deciding to use *self* exclusively to refer to the *ātman, psyche, soul,* or that core of our being that I have argued to be illusory. And I am deciding to use the word *person* to refer to the actual entity in which I will argue our reality consists. Others use these terms differently, but I think that this regimentation will permit us some clarity that would be harder to achieve otherwise. And there is good philosophical precedent—in India and in the West—for this usage.

2. If Jaini (1979, 101) is correct, the etymology of *pudgala* is also useful. Although this is controversial, Jaini argues that it is a compound that means *to come together and to disintegrate,* an etymology reflected in the Tibetan translation as *'jig tshogs,* or *transitory collection.* So, this suggests that while an *ātman* is supposed to be an unchanging core, a *pudgala* is a constantly changing sequence.

3. Tsongkhapa argues that one criterion for the reality of an entity is for there to be a difference between truth and falsity with regard to that entity. Note here that just as there is a difference between truth and falsity with regard to the actor, there is with regard to the character. We can get it right or wrong about Hamlet, and we can also be right or wrong about Cumberbatch; and it is facts about Hamlet the character that determine whether we are right or wrong about him, and facts about Cumberbatch that determine whether we are right or wrong about him. A second criterion Tsongkhapa endorses is causal efficacy. Real things have causes and effects. Once again, although their causes and effects are different, actor and character each have causes, and each have effects. Cumberbatch might cause me to see what is happening on stage when he plays Hamlet, but it is Hamlet, not Cumberbatch, who causes me to consider the meaning of my life. So, both characters and actors satisfy each of these criteria for reality. For these reasons, if we follow Tsongkhapa's reasoning, each is real, although in different contexts.

4. See Hutto's *Narrative and Understanding Persons* (2007), Sorabji's *Self: Ancient and Modern Insights about Individuality, Life, and Death* (2006), and Farouque's *Sculpting the Self* (2021) for extended discussions of the role of narrative in the construction of the person. We will return to the sense in which and the mechanisms by means of which this identity emerges in chapters 7 and 8.

5. A good deal of contemporary feminist theory and race theory attends to these issues. But to address them in the context of a Buddhist account of interdependence and selflessness, see Gross, *Buddhism beyond Gender* (2018) as well as Yancy and McRae, *Buddhism and Whiteness* (2019).

Chapter 4

1. For a detailed discussion of this argument, see Chakrabarti, "I Touch What I Saw," *Philosophy and Phenomenological Research* 52:1 (1992), pp. 103–16.

2. See Ganeri, *The Self: Naturalism, Consciousness, and the First-Person Stance* (1992), p. 58, and Sorabji (1996), chapter 12.

3. The difference between action and attribute is unimportant here, and both kinds of language occur in Indian and European formulations of the argument.

4. Kant, for instance, argued that the fact that geometric truths, such as that the interior angles of a triangle add up to 180 degrees, are necessarily true and can be known by reasoning alone demonstrates that space is projected by the mind as a structure in which to represent external objects. Otherwise, he argued, geometric knowledge would be empirical, learned through experience, like our knowledge that apples are red, and so possibly false.

This transcendental argument takes as its *explanandum* the fact that geometrical truths can be known with certainty, cannot be false, and can be known by reason alone. Kant then argues that this would not be true if space and the spatiality of objects existed independent of our minds, and so he concludes that the only *explanans* for the status of geometric truths is the fact that space is a projection of our minds, as he puts it, *the form of outer sense*. (For present purposes, neither the details of that argument nor its success or failure are important; I present it only as a clear instance of this form of argument.)

5. By *synchronic* unity, once again, we mean the unity of subjective experience in each moment, or the experience that I am a single subject of all that I now experience. By *diachronic* unity, we mean our identity over time.

6. This so-called argument from design crops up frequently in the history of Western philosophy. It is the basis of "natural theology." Hume subjects it to extensive critique in his *Dialogues Concerning Natural Religion*.

7. Ganeri discusses the binding problem and its role in classical Indian discussions of the self in great detail in *The Self: Naturalism, Consciousness and the First-Person Stance* (2012), pp. 188–99, 288–92. See Metzinger, *Being No-One: The Self-Theory Model of Subjectivity* (2004), chapter 3, for a discussion of that problem from the perspective of contemporary philosophy of mind and neuroscience, and for an argument that one cannot get from the reality of cognitive binding to the reality of a self that does that binding. For a careful discussion of debates in India between Buddhist and orthodox philosophers regarding the existence of the *ātman*, see Watson, "Self or No-Self: The Ātman Debate in Classical Indian Philosophy" (2017).

8. For examples, see Gallagher and Zahavi, *The Phenomenological Mind* (2012); Kriegel, *The Varieties of Consciousness* (2018); Thompson, *Mind in Life: Biology, Phenomenology, and the Sciences of Mind* (2010), *Waking, Dreaming, Being: Self and*

Consciousness in Neuroscience, Meditation, and Philosophy (2014), and *Why I Am Not a Buddhist* (2020); and Zahavi, *Subjectivity and Selfhood: Investigating the First-Person Perspective* (2008), and *Self-Awareness and Alterity: A Phenomenological Investigation* (2020).

9. We find similar arguments in the Vedānta tradition, and especially in the Kantian neo-Vedānta tradition that flourished in India in the late nineteenth and early twentieth centuries. See Bhushan and Garfield, *Minds without Fear* (2017), chapter 11, for a discussion, and Mukerji, *The Nature of Self* (1938) and Bhattacharyya, *Subject as Freedom* (1930) for fine examples. Also see Sorabji, *Self: Ancient and Modern Insights about Individuality, Life, And Death* (2012), chapter 14, for a detailed discussion of these issues.

10. Dennett makes this point eloquently in *Consciousness Explained* (1992).

11. *Being No-One: The Self-Theory of Model of Subjectivity* (2004), chapter 4.

12. Ibid., pp. 627–29.

13. We find this argument in the classical Indian Nyāya school. It is discussed in some Buddhist epistemological literature in India, and in the West in the work of Kant and of Edmund Husserl (1859–1938) . See the first and second analogies of experience in Kant's *Critique of Pure Reason* (1999) and Husserl's *Phenomenology of Internal Time Consciousness* (1964).

14. Śāntideva develops this argument in chapter 9 of *How to Lead an Awakened Life*. I discuss it in Garfield (2006). Evan Thompson replies in (2011) and (2020).

15. For a more extensive treatment of these arguments from the unity of the subject or the object to the reality of the self, see Ganeri, *The Self: Naturalism, Consciousness, and the First-Person Stance* (2012), especially chapter 15.

Chapter 5

1. These arguments are from Strawson, "Radical Self-Awareness" (2011a); from Zahavi, *Subjectivity and Selfhood: Investigating the First-Person Perspective* (2008); and from Zahavi, *Self-Awareness and Alterity: A Phenomenological Investigation* (2020).

2. Strawson (2011a), p. 276.

3. Ibid., 279.

4. We will address this claim more directly in a short while, but for now it is interesting to note that the Buddhist philosophers who criticize this view—prominently including philosophers in the Madhyamaka, or Middle Way School, including Candrakīrti, Śāntideva, and Tsongkhapa—criticize it in part on the grounds that it ends up entailing a commitment to the self. The fact that the reflexivity thesis is mobilized in contemporary defenses of the reality of the self confirms that their critique was on target. For a discussion of this literature on reflexivity, see Garfield, "The Conventional Status of Reflexive Awareness: What's at Stake in a

Tibetan Debate?" (2006), and Williams, *The Reflexive Nature of Awareness: A Tibetan Madhyamaka Defence* (2000). See also Ganeri, *The Self: Naturalism, Consciousness, and the First-Person Stance* (2012), chapter 9.

5. Strawson (2011a), pp. 279–80.

6. See Ganeri, *Attention, Not Self* (2017), and Thompson, *Mind in Life: Biology, Phenomenology, and the Sciences of Mind* (2010), for two very different accounts of this view of attention and awareness.

7. Heidegger is often seen as the forerunner of this view. For a Heideggerian exposition of this position, see Haugeland, *Dasein Disclosed* (2013). See also Paul Churchland, *The Engine of Reason, the Seat of the Soul* (1996), Owen Flanagan, *Consciousness Reconsidered* (1992), Nisbett and Ross (1980), and Schwitzgebel (2011) for a variety of distinct defenses of illusionism. Jan Westerhoff, in *The Non-Existence of the Real World* (2020), argues persuasively for the illusory nature of the self in the context of a more general argument for the conclusion that everything we ever experience is illusory. His arguments, however, target prominent arguments for the reality of the self directly. For a nice set of papers on illusionism, see Frankish (2017).

8. There is what philosophers call a *de dicto/de re* ambiguity here, but that doesn't help Strawson. While my awareness of the flash of red might be an awareness of the cardinal *de re*, it is not of the cardinal *de dicto*. And to characterize the contents of consciousness, it is *de dicto* descriptions that matter.

9. Strawson's most extensive argument for the existence of selves, of which this discussion is but a part, is presented in his book *Selves* (2011b). A complete discussion of all of the arguments in that book is well beyond the scope of this volume. But the central claims and inferences advanced in that book are those discussed here.

10. Thompson, "Self-No-Self: Memory and Reflexive Awareness" (2011), pp. 157–75.

11. It is this argument that Candrakīrti had in mind when he argued that this doctrine leads inevitably to the reintroduction through the back door of the self that Buddhist philosophers had taken such pains to evict through the front door. While Dignāga and his followers deny that the reflexivity thesis entails the commitment to the self, and so take it to be compatible with Buddhist no-self theory, Candrakīrti, Śāntideva, Tsongkhapa, and their followers argue that it does entail the reality of a self. This generates a long intramural dispute in Buddhist epistemology regarding reflexivity. See Williams, *The Reflexive Nature of Awareness: A Tibetan Madhyamaka Defence* (2000) for a careful treatment of this debate.

12. See Loftus, *Memory: Surprising New Insights into How We Remember and Why We Forget* (1988).

13. I address this issue at length in Garfield (2006).

14. See Ganeri, *The Self: Naturalism, Consciousness, and the First-Person Stance* (2002), pp. 174–81, for a perceptive discussion of Indian Buddhist and Western

arguments for the reflexivity of awareness and the difficulties that plague them, both on their own terms and as arguments for the reality of the self.

15. This is so despite the fact that many who defend a minimal or narrative self deny that they are committed to this kind of self. Part of the motivation of these apparently less metaphysically rich conceptions of the self is to retain the *mine* without the *I* (e.g., Zahavi, "The Experiential Self: Objections and Clarifications" [2011], pp. 64–71). But the attempt must fail: to the extent that the ownership of experience is taken as essential to experience, the owner must be as well, even if it is shrunken to a point. This is why Wittgenstein's metaphor of the eye and the visual field is so helpful. Even when we exclude the eye from the visual field, we nonetheless presuppose its existence, and indeed its foundational status.

16. Zahavi (2011), 58.

17. Ibid., 59.

18. This is what is wrong with the idea introduced by Nagel (1974) in "What Is It Like to Be a Bat?" (*The Philosophical Review* 83:4, pp. 435–50) that there is "something that it is like" to be a bat, or a person. This confuses the idea that there is something that, e.g., a mosquito is like for a bat that detects it by echolocation vs. for a person who detects it by vision and hearing, with the idea that there is something that bat subjectivity is like, or person-subjectivity. Or to take an analogy of Wittgenstein's in *On Certainty* (1969), we know perfectly well what it is to be noon in New York, or in Los Angeles. So, we might think that we know what it is to be noon on the sun. But that makes no sense at all. Similarly, from the fact that we tell whether some object, e.g., a watch, is mine or yours by inspecting it and searching for some identifying property, it might appear that we also tell whether an experience is mine or yours by searching for an identifying property. But the analogy simply crumbles. *For-me-ness* appears to make sense; it does not.

19. See Krueger, "The Who and the How of Experience" (2011). Wittgenstein makes a similar point in *Philosophical Investigations* (2009), ¶ 308.

20. It is worth recalling the fact that even the *cogito* argument only gives us our existence and our nature as thinking things at the moment we are thinking.

21. Ganeri, in *The Self: Naturalism, Consciousness, and the First-Person Stance* (2012), chapters 6 and 8, levels a similar charge against Zahavi. Ganeri, however, agrees with Zahavi that our own experiences do exhibit *mineness* or *for-me-ness*. He just doesn't think that this entails the reality of a self. Metzinger defends a similar view in *Being No-One: The Self-Theory Model of Subjectivity* (2004), chapter 6.

22. Thompson presents this account as a reconstruction of the classical Indian Buddhist view that all awareness is reflexive. There is reason to debate that interpretation. But whether or not this is exegetically correct is beside the present point.

23. Thompson, "Self-No-Self: Memory and Reflexive Awareness" (2011), pp. 158–59.

24. Thompson might respond that the awareness of a self is always *intransitive*, while one's awareness of one's identity as a person is always *transitive*. But to stipulate this would be to beg the question in this context, and it is hard to see how one could argue for this distinction. After all, it has to be true that persons see apples, and if seeing an apple is what discloses a subject, that subject could just as well be a person as a self.

25. The argument found in *Being No-One: The Self-Theory Model of Subjectivity* (2004).

26. *Why I Am Not a Buddhist* (2020), p. 106.

27. Ibid., p. 111.

28. Ibid., p. 112.

29. Ibid., p. 113.

30. See his *Narrative and Understanding Persons* (2007). Although Hutto is the most prominent contemporary exponent of this view, it does not originate with him. See Ricoeur, *Oneself as Another* (1995), fifth and sixth studies, as well as Alasdair McIntyre, *After Virtue* (1985) chapter 15, for important antecedents.

31. Krueger makes the point persuasively in "The Who and the How of Experience" (2011), pp. 34–37.

32. Daniel Dennett, in *Consciousness Explained* (1992), argues that the self is a fictional center of narrative gravity en route to an account of the nature of consciousness. While he is not primarily concerned with the status of the self, or of the distinction between the self and the person that I have thematized here, his account does demonstrate the perils of not drawing this distinction carefully. It is one thing to say that as persons we are constructed by narratives; but the thing that we grasp as a self is grasped not through narrative, but through instinctual capitulation to cognitive illusion.

Chapter 6

1. Translation from Watson (1964), 50–51. I have changed the translation of the character that Watson reads as *cook* to *butcher,* both because it is a more common reading of the text, and because it makes much more sense of the final line of the text. I have also converted the names to Pinyin transliteration. Robert Sharf notes (personal communication) that the title of the text *Pao Ding jie niu,* or *Cook/Butcher Ding Carves an Ox, pao,* has a range of meanings, and that this term in particular could be read as kitchen, cuisine, and cook, but does appear in lexicons as "butcher," probably from this particular anecdote. Sharf also notes that the basic meaning of *jie* is to untie, unravel, and thus release. It comes to mean *explicate* (as in *parse* or *analyze* a text), but also *liberate.* So in this anecdote it means to cut apart, but (just for fun) it could also be translated *Cook Ding Liberates the Ox* or *Cook Ding Explicates the Ox.*

2. Mihalyi Csikszentmihalyi introduced this term. His book *Flow: The Psychology of Optimal Experience* (1990) provides an excellent exposition. For a detailed exploration of the relationship between Chinese philosophical accounts of effortless action (*wu wei*) and the contemporary psychological discussion of flow, see Slingerland (2007).

3. For more on this story, see Deguchi, Garfield, Priest, and Sharf, *What Can't Be Said: Paradox and Contradiction in East Asian Thought* (2021, chapter 2), and Garfield and Priest, "Upāya and Spontaneity: Skill and Expertise in Daoist and Buddhist Traditions," (2020), pp. 29–39. See also Haugeland's account of Heidegger's discussion of absorbed coping in *Dasein Disclosed* (2013) for a more European version of the same idea.

4. See Moulton and Epstein, "Self-Monitoring in Surgical Practice: Slowing Down When You Should" (2005). See the discussion on p. 171.

5. Ibid., p. 173.

6. Ibid., p. 174.

7. See Beilock and Carr, "From Novice to Expert Performance: Memory, Attention, and the Control of Complex Motor Skills" (2004).

8. See Noice and Noice, "Artistic Performance: Acting, Ballet, and Contemporary Dance" (2006).

9. See N. Hodges, J. Starkes, and C. MacMahon, "Expert Performance in Sport: A Cognitive Perspective" (2006), and D. Rosenbaum et al., "Perceptual-Motor Expertise" (2006).

10. Translation by R. Aitken and K. Tanahashi in *Moon in a Dewdrop: Writings of Zen Master Dōgen* (1995), p. 70.

11. Indeed, Metzinger and his associates showed that is possible to induce a full-body version of the "rubber-hand" illusion. In the basic illusion, it is possible to produce the sense that a visual simulation of one's hand is indeed one's hand. Metzinger shows that we can create a virtual reality illusion in which one locates one's entire bodily subjectivity in a virtual body, demonstrating the complex, porous relationship between body and subjectivity (*The Ego Tunnel: The Science of the Mind and the Myth of the Self* [2010], pp. 98–101). While we might think that our body is essential to our identity, we can not only imagine ourselves to have a different body, as the thought experiment in the first chapter showed, but we can even *believe* ourselves to have a different one in the right circumstances!

Chapter 7

1. *A Theory of Justice* (1999).

2. For various instances of this point in contemporary Western ethical theory, see Baier, *The Moral Point of View* (1966), Nagel, *The View from Nowhere* (1989), and Rawls, *A Theory of Justice* (1999), among many others.

3. See Dalai Lama, *Ethics for the New Millennium* (1999), *Ethics for the Whole World* (2011), and *Practicing Wisdom: The Perfection of Shantideva's Bodhisattva Way* (2012), as well as Thich Nhat Hanh's *Interbeing* (1987), *Love in Action: Writings on Nonviolent Social Change* (1993), *Being Peace* (2005), and *The Art of Living: Peace and Freedom in the Here and Now* (2017) for fine discussions of the relevance of selflessness and of the nature of personhood to ethical consciousness.

4. It is for this reason that many scholars (myself included) now opt to translate *karuṇā* as *care*, rather than as *compassion*, as it was translated for many years. This gets at the fact that the attitude is not just a feeling, let alone a feeling of another's pain, but rather a commitment to act on someone's behalf to relieve their suffering.

5. For a more extensive discussion of the divine states, see Bommarito, *Seeing Clearly: A Buddhist Guide to Life* (2020), chapter 26; Garfield, *Buddhist Ethics: A Philosophical Exploration* (2021), chapter 9; Gowans, *Buddhist Moral Theory: An Introduction* (2017); and Heim, *Buddhist Ethics* (2020).

6. See also Parfit, *Reasons and Persons* (1984), for an extended inquiry into the relationship between no-self and ethics.

7. I discuss this connection between freedom and the illusion of self at greater length in "Just Another Word for Nothing Left to Lose: Freedom, Agency and Ethics for Mādhyamikas" (2014), and in *Buddhist Ethics: A Philosophical Exploration* (2021), chapter 4.

8. Translation my own, from the Tibetan edition.

9. Peter Strawson, in "Freedom and Resentment" (in P. F. Strawson, *Freedom and Resentment and Other Essays*, 2008, pp. 1–28), Bernard Williams (in *Ethics and the Limits of Philosophy*, 1986), and Stephen Darwall (in *The Second-Person Standpoint: Morality, Respect, and Accountability*, 2009) have each, in very different ways, emphasized the role of what Strawson dubbed the "reactive attitudes" in our understanding of moral standing, both of ourselves and others. It is worth noting that while Śāntideva would reject the probity of many of the reactive attitudes that some or all of these contemporary theorists valorize, he would agree that certain reactive attitudes must be cultivated as part of the process of moral development. But attitudes such as anger and resentment would not be part of Śāntideva's recommended portfolio. For an exploration of the utility of anger in the context of a Buddhist account of selfless agency, see McRae, "Metabolizing Anger: A Tantric Buddhist Solution to the Problem of Moral Anger" (2015), and "Anger and the Oppressed: Indo-Tibetan Buddhist Perspectives" (2018).

10. One might worry that this perspective undermines attributions of moral responsibility: if all of our actions are caused by previous events, one might argue, this means that we are never responsible for what we do, and that praise, blame, guilt, and other such attitudes of moral appraisal make no sense. This intuition is often used to motivate a commitment to Augustinian freedom. But this does not follow. Instead,

we should rethink the basis of these attitudes. They need not rest on an attribution of absolute freedom, but instead on the recognition of the kinds of psychological causes that motivate behavior, and on the personal narratives that make sense of the lives in the context of which actions occur. Attitudes of moral appraisal are important, and reflect our individual or collective approval and disapproval of actions, attitudes, states of character, etc. They reflect our interpretations of ourselves and others, and to abandon such appraisal would be to fail to treat others and ourselves as *persons*. But nothing follows from the cogency and utility of these moral practices regarding freedom from causation. If this were required, moral appraisal would indeed make no sense.

Chapter 8

1. Even readopting a gold standard or reintroducing silver certificates would not change this fact: it would only postpone the question to one about precious metals.

2. This was the approach of some twentieth-century logical positivists, and proponents of the "unity of science" thesis such as Rudolf Carnap, Hilary Putnam, and Ernest Nagel. It is a view that has fallen out of favor as a richer understanding of the relationship between the sciences has emerged.

3. For more on supervenience and the reality and independence of the mental, see Davidson, "Mental Events" (2001), in D. Davidson, *Essays on Actions and Events*, pp. 207–28, Garfield, *Belief in Psychology* (1988), Baker, *Saving Belief* (2017), and the essays in part I of Kim, *Supervenience and Mind* (2008). For a spirited defense of reductionism as an account of personhood in the context of no-self, drawing on both classical Buddhist and contemporary Western philosophy, see Siderits, *Personal Identity and Buddhist Philosophy: Empty Persons* (2017).

4. Ganeri, in *The Self: Naturalism, Consciousness, and the First-Person Stance* (2012), pp. 77–82, reminds us that supervenience theories were well known and were debated in classical and medieval Indian philosophy. Nyāya-Vaiśeṣika and Cārvāka theorists each defended supervenience theories of the mental, although they are slightly different from one another. On the other hand, while the Nyāya-Vaiśeṣika system is committed to the reality of the *ātman*, the Cārvākas were materialists. It is, however, unclear whether, like the Buddhists, they rejected the self entirely, or affirmed that the body is the self. It is also worth noting that Buddhist philosophers in India rejected the supervenience of the mental on the physical, and indeed on some readings, some Yogācāra Buddhist philosophers might even have taken the physical to supervene on the mental.

5. Tolman, "Physiology, Psychology, and Sociology" (1938), p. 227.

6. Sellars, "Empiricism and the Philosophy of Mind" (1963).

7. To read more about how language shapes thought, see Lakoff, *Women, Fire, and Dangerous Things: What Categories Reveal about the Mind* (1990); Lakoff and Johnson, *Metaphors We Live By* (2003); and Boroditsky, "Metaphoric Structuring: Understanding Time through Spatial Metaphors" (2000), "Does Language Shape Thought? Mandarin and English Speakers' Conceptions of Time" (2001), and "Time in the Mind: Using Space to Think about Time" (2008).

8. Tolman, "Physiology, Psychology, and Sociology" (1938), p. 231.

9. For those interested in Reddy's work, I recommend "On Being the Object of Attention: Implications for Self-Other Consciousness"(2003), "Getting Back to the Rough Ground: Deception and 'Social Living'" (2007), "Engagement: Looking beyond the Mirror to Understand Action Understanding" (2016), and "Why Engagement? A Second-Person Take on Social Cognition" (2018).

10. Reddy's program is very much in the spirit of the work of the twentieth-century psychologist Lev Vygotsky (1896–1934), who emphasized the role of joint activity, cooperative play, and the support of others, as well as cultural context, in scaffolding learning in what he called the "zone of proximal development." Vygotsky also argued, in *Mind in Society: The Development of Higher Psychological Processes* (1978), as does Reddy, for the spontaneity of our interpretation of behavior as intentional, and for the role of dyadic interactions and of playful activity in the emergence of self-consciousness. Also see Sharf, "Ritual" (2005), and Garfield, Peterson, and Perry, "Social Cognition, Language Acquisition and the Development of the Theory of Mind" (2001), for more on Vygotskyan accounts of development. Reddy's experimental work both confirms the utility of that theoretical framework and represents a detailed application of that framework to the study of the origins of self-knowledge.

11. "On Being the Object of Attention: Implications for Self-Other Consciousness" (2003), p. 397.

12. Ibid.

13. Reddy, "Engagement: Looking beyond the Mirror to Understand Action Understanding" (2016).

14. See also Carpendale and Lewis (2004, 2006, 2010) for additional evidence for these phenomena. They also emphasize the importance of early dyadic interactions for the development both of social intelligence and of self-understanding.

15. This is long before "theory of mind" emerges in the fourth year of life, as measured by passing false belief tasks, and well before the acquisition of competence with the semantics or syntax of sentential complement clauses that enable children to succeed at these tasks, suggesting an important dichotomy between implicit and explicit theory of mind (de Villiers and de Villiers 1999; Garfield, Peterson, and Perry 2001; Fenici 2012, 2017a, 2017b).

16. Reddy, "Why Engagement? A Second-Person Take on Social Cognition" (2018), pp. 433–34.

17. Ibid., p. 438.

18. There are dozens of studies that confirm this result. Here are a few. Grossman, Parise, and Friederici (2010), using near-infrared spectroscopy (NIRS), found that specific adjacent areas of the prefrontal cortex are active in infants in response to communicative intention from adults, one area that responds to eye contact and one to the use of the infant's name; this response is subserved by a common area in older children and adults. Farroni, Csibra, Simion, and Johnson (2002) used an ERP study to show that specific neural activity responds to eye contact in two-to-five-day-old infants. Grossman, Johnson, Farroni, and Csibra (2007) show that specific gamma band oscillation in infant brains responds to eye contact from human faces. Turning to adults, Kampe, Frith, and Frith (2003) find that hearing one's own name activates the paracingulate cortex and temporal poles, areas closely associated with the attribution of mental states to others; Hietanen and Hietanen (2017) find that eye contact with a genuine interlocutor increases self-awareness and the use of first-person pronouns.

19. Note, for instance, how effective Śāntideva's and Patrul's prose is in virtue of their forceful use of the second person. For another example of very effective use of the second person in Buddhist ethical writing, see Patrul Rinpoche (2017). Thanks to Emily McRae for pointing this out.

20. Reddy (2018), pp. 439–42.

Chapter 9

1. See Wittgenstein, *Philosophical Investigations* (2009); Sellars, "Some Reflections on Language Games" (1954), and "Language as Thought and as Communication" (1969); and Kripke, *Wittgenstein on Rules and Private Language* (1991).

2. *Enquiry Concerning the Human Understanding*, 4.24.

3. I explore these ideas in the context of Hume's philosophy in *The Concealed Influence of Custom: Hume's "Treatise" from the Inside Out* (2019). See especially chapters 2 and 13.

4. Sellars makes this point forcefully in "Empiricism and the Philosophy of Mind" (1963).

5. To see where these ideas about the interrelations between the first, second, and third person originate, see Bhattacharyya, *Subject as Freedom* (1930).

6. This point is made forcefully by Davidson in "Mental Events" (2001), by Haugeland in *Dasein Disclosed* (2013), and by Dennett in *The Intentional Stance* (1989).

7. See Hutto, *Narrative and Understanding Persons* (2007), and Thompson, *Why I Am Not a Buddhist* (2020).

8. See also Kusch, "The Sociophilosophy of Folk Psychology" (1997), for a defense of this account of self-understanding in terms of interpretation.

9. See *The Conscious Mind: In Search of a Fundamental Theory* (1997).

10. Stephen Darwall has developed this insight with great care and depth in his account of second-person ethics in *The Second-Person Standpoint: Morality, Respect, and Accountability* (2009), and in *Morality, Authority, and the Law: Essays on Second-Personal Ethics I* (2013).

11. One way to put this point is to note that even to recognize someone as saying something false requires that we also recognize them as generally speaking the truth. To take someone to disagree with us about some matter requires that we also take them to agree with us on a host of other matters. Otherwise, we would have no confidence that we are interpreting what they say correctly, and no basis for ascribing a false utterance to them. See Davidson, "Mental Events" (2001).

12. For an extended discussion of Śāntideva's arguments in chapter 8 of *How to Lead an Awakened Life*, see Cowherds, *Moonpaths: Ethics and Emptiness* (2015).

REFERENCES

Anacker, A. 2015. *Seven Works of Vasubandhu: The Buddhist Psychological Doctor.* New Delhi: Motilal Banarsidass.

Baier, K. 1966. *The Moral Point of View.* Ithaca: Cornell University Press.

Baker, L. R. 2017. *Saving Belief: A Critique of Physicalism.* Princeton: Princeton University Press.

Becker, E. 1997. *The Denial of Death.* New York: The Free Press.

Beckwith, C. 2015. *Greek Buddha: Pyrrho's Encounter with Buddhism in Central Asia.* Princeton, NJ: Princeton University Press.

Beilock, S., and T. Carr. 2004. "From Novice to Expert Performance: Memory, Attention, and the Control of Complex Motor Skills." In N. Hodges, ed., *Skill Acquisition in Sport: Research, Theory and Practice.* London: Routledge, pp. 309–27.

Bhattacharyya, K. C. 1930. *Subject as Freedom.* Amalner: Indian Council for Philosophical Research.

Bhushan, N. and J. Garfield. 2017. *Minds without Fear: Philosophy in the Indian Renaissance.* New York: Oxford University Press.

Bommarito, N. 2020. *Seeing Clearly: A Buddhist Guide to Life.* New York: Oxford University Press.

Boroditsky, L. 2000. "Metaphoric Structuring: Understanding Time through Spatial Metaphors." *Cognition* 75:1, pp. 1–28.

———. 2001. "Does Language Shape Thought? Mandarin and English Speakers' Conceptions of Time." *Cognitive Psychology* 43:1, pp. 1–22.

———. 2008. "Time in the Mind: Using Space to Think about Time." *Cognition* 106:2, pp. 579–93.

Bradley, F. H. 1893. *Appearance and Reality.* London: Allen and Unwin.

Carpendale, J., and C. Lewis. 2004. "Constructing an Understanding of Mind: the Development of Children's Social Understanding Within Social Interaction." *Behavioral and Brain Sciences* 27:1, pp. 79–96.

———. 2006. *How Children Develop Social Understanding.* Malden: Blackwell.

————. 2010. "The Development of Social Understanding: A Relational Perspective." In R. Lerner, ed., *The Handbook of Life-Span Development*. Hoboken: John Wiley and Sons.

Chakrabarti, A. 1992. "I Touch What I Saw." *Philosophy and Phenomenological Research* 52:1, pp. 103–16.

Chalmers, D. 1997. *The Conscious Mind: In Search of a Fundamental Theory*. Oxford: Oxford University Press.

Chandrakīrti and Mipham. 2005. "*Introduction to the Middle Way*": Chandrakirti's *Madhyamakavatara with Commentary by Ju Mipham*. Boston: Shambhala.

Churchland, P. 1996. *The Engine of Reason, the Seat of the Soul*. Cambridge: MIT Press.

Collins, S. 2008. *Selfless Persons*. Cambridge: Cambridge University Press.

Cowherds. 2015. *Moonpaths: Ethics and Emptiness*. New York: Oxford University Press.

Crosby, K., and A. Skilton. 2014. *Śāntideva: "The Bodhicāryāvatāra.*" Oxford: Oxford University Press.

Csikszentmihalyi, M. 1990. *Flow: The Psychology of Optimal Experience*. New York: Harper.

Dalai Lama. 1999. *Ethics for the New Millennium*. New York: Riverhead Books.

————. 2011. *Ethics for the Whole World*. New York: Mariner Books.

————. 2012. *Practicing Wisdom: The Perfection of Shantideva's Bodhisattva Way*. New York: Simon and Schuster.

Damasio, A. 2000. *The Feeling of What Happens*. New York: Mariner Books.

Darwall, S. 2009. *The Second-Person Standpoint: Morality, Respect, and Accountability*. Cambridge, MA: Harvard University Press.

————. 2013. *Morality, Authority, and the Law: Essays on Second-Personal Ethics I*. Oxford: Oxford University Press.

Davidson, D. 2001. "Mental Events." In D. Davidson, *Essays on Actions and Events*. Oxford: Clarendon Press, pp. 207–28.

Deguchi, Y., J. Garfield, G. Priest, and R. Sharf. 2021. *What Can't Be Said: Paradox and Contradiction in East Asian Thought*. New York: Oxford University Press.

Dennett, D. 1984. *Elbow Room: Varieties of Freedom Worth Wanting*. Cambridge, MA: MIT Press/Bradford Books.

————. 1989. *The Intentional Stance*. Cambridge, MA: MIT Press/Bradford Books.

————. 1992. *Consciousness Explained*. New York: Little Brown and Co.

de Villiers, J., and de Villiers, P. 1999. "Linguistic Determinism and the Understanding of False Beliefs." In P. Mitchell and K. Riggs, eds., *Children's Reasoning and the Mind*. New York: Psychology Press, pp. 191–228.

Dōgen. 1995. *Moon in a Dewdrop: Writings of Zen Master Dōgen*. Trans. K. Tanahashi and R. Aitken. San Francisco: North Point Press

Edelglass, W., and J. Garfield, eds. 2009. *Buddhist Philosophy: Essential Readings.* New York: Oxford University Press.

Ericsson, K. A., N. Charness, R. Hoffman, and P. Feltovich, eds. 2006. *The Cambridge Handbook of Expertise and Expert Performance.* Cambridge: Cambridge University Press.

Farouque, M. 2021. *Sculpting the Self.* Ann Arbor: University of Michigan Press.

Farroni, T., G. Csibra, F. Simion, and M. Johnson. 2002. "Eye Contact Detection in Humans from Birth." *Proceedings of the National Academy of Sciences* 9:14, pp. 9602–5.

Fenici, M. 2012. "Embodied Social Cognition and Embedded Theory of Mind." *Biolinguistics* 6, pp. 276–307.

———. 2017a. "What Is the Role of Experience in Children's Success in the False Belief Task: Maturation, Facilitation, Attunement, or Induction?" *Mind and Language* 32:3, pp. 308–37.

———. 2017b. "The Biocultural Emergence of Mindreading: Integrating Cognitive Archaeology and Human Development." *Journal of Cultural Cognitive Science* 1:2, pp. 89–117.

Flanagan, O. 1992. *Consciousness Reconsidered.* Cambridge: MIT Press.

———. 2002. *The Problem of the Soul.* New York: Basic Books.

Frankish, K., ed. 2017. *Illusionism.* London: Imprint Academic.

Gallagher, S., and D. Zahavi. 2012. *The Phenomenological Mind.* London: Routledge.

Ganeri, J. 2012. *The Self: Naturalism, Consciousness, and the First-Person Stance.* Oxford: Oxford University Press.

Ganeri, J. 2017. *Attention, Not Self.* Oxford: Oxford University Press.

Garfield, J. 1988. *Belief in Psychology: A Study in the Ontology of Mind.* Cambridge, MA: MIT Press/Bradford Books.

———. 1990. "*Epoché* and *Śūnyatā*: Skepticism East and West." *Philosophy East and West* 40:3, pp. 285–307.

———. 2006. "The Conventional Status of Reflexive Awareness: What's at Stake in a Tibetan Debate?" *Philosophy East and West* 56:3, pp. 201–28.

———. 2014. "Just Another Word for Nothing Left to Lose: Freedom, Agency and Ethics for Mādhyamikas." In M. Dasti and E. Bryant, eds., *Freedom of the Will in a Cross-Cultural Perspective.* New York: Oxford University Press, pp. 164–85.

———. 2015. *Engaging Buddhism: Why It Matters to Philosophy.* New York: Oxford University Press.

———. 2019. *The Concealed Influence of Custom: Hume's "Treatise" from the Inside Out.* New York: Oxford University Press.

———. 2021. *Buddhist Ethics: A Philosophical Exploration.* New York: Oxford University Press.

Garfield, J., C. Peterson, and T. Perry. 2001. "Social Cognition, Language Acquisition and the Development of the Theory of Mind." *Mind and Language* 15:5, pp. 445–91.

Garfield, J., and G. Priest. 2020. "Upāya and Spontaneity: Skill and Expertise in Daoist and Buddhist Traditions." In E. Fridland and C. Pavese, eds., *The Routledge Handbook of Skill and Expertise.* London: Routledge, pp. 29–39.

Gowans, C. 2017. *Buddhist Moral Theory: An Introduction.* London: Routledge.

Gross, R. 2018. *Buddhism beyond Gender.* Boston: Shambhala.

Grossman, T., M. Johnson, T. Farroni, and G. Csibra. 2007. "Social Perception in the Infant Brain: Gamma Oscillatory Activity in Response to Eye Gaze." *Social Cognitive and Affective Neuroscience* 2, pp. 284–91.

Grossman, T., E. Parise, and A. Friederici. 2010. "The Detection of Communicative Signals Directed at the Self in the Infant Prefrontal Cortex." *Frontiers in Neuroscience* 4, pp. 1–5.

Haugeland, J. 2013. *Dasein Disclosed.* Cambridge, MA: Harvard University Press.

Heim, M. 2020. *Buddhist Ethics.* Cambridge: Cambridge University Press.

Hietanen, H., and H. Hietanen. 2017. "Genuine Eye Contact Elicits Self-Referential Processing." *Consciousness and Cognition* 51, pp. 100–115.

Hodges, N., J. Starkes, and C. MacMahon. 2006. "Expert Performance in Sport: A Cognitive Perspective." In Ericsson, et al. (2006), pp. 471–88.

Horner, I. B. 1964. *The Questions of King Milinda.* Bristol: Pali Text Society.

Huntington, C. W., and Namgyal Wangchen. 1995. *The Emptiness of Emptiness.* Honolulu: University of Hawai'i Press.

Husserl, E. 1964. *The Phenomenology of Internal Time Consciousness.* Bloomington: Indiana University Press.

Hutto, D. 2007. *Narrative and Understanding Persons.* Cambridge: Cambridge University Press.

Iqbal, M. 2020. *The Reconstruction of Religious Thought in Islam.* New Delhi: Kitab Bhavan.

Jaini, P. S. 1979. *The Jaina Path of Purification.* New Delhi: Motilal Banarsidass.

Kampe, K., C. Frith, and U. Frith. 2003. "'Hey John': Signals Conveying Communication towards the Self Activate Brain Regions Associated with 'Mentalizing,' Regardless of Modality." *Journal of Neuroscience* 23:12, pp. 5258–63.

Kant, I. 1999. *The Critique of Pure Reason.* Cambridge: Cambridge University Press.

Kenny, A. 1988. *The Self.* Milwaukee: Marquette University Press.

Kim, J. 2008. *Supervenience and Mind.* Cambridge: Cambridge University Press.

Kochumuttom, T. 2008. *A Buddhist Doctrine of Experience: A New Translation and Interpretation of the Works of Vasubandhu.* New Delhi: Motilal Banarsidass.

Kriegel, U. 2018. *The Varieties of Consciousness.* Oxford: Oxford University Press.

Kripke, S. 1991. *Wittgenstein on Rules and Private Language*. Cambridge, MA: Harvard University Press.

Krueger, J. 2011. "The Who and the How of Experience." In Siderits, Thompson, and Zavahi (2011), pp. 27–55.

Kusch, M. 1997. "The Sociophilosophy of Folk Psychology." *Studies in the History and Philosophy of Science* 28, pp. 1–25.

Kuzminski, A. 2008. *Pyrrhonism: How the Ancient Greeks Reinvented Buddhism*. Lanham, MD: Lexington Books.

Lakoff, G. 1990. *Women, Fire, and Dangerous Things: What Categories Reveal about the Mind*. Chicago: University of Chicago Press.

Lakoff, G., and M. Johnson. 2003. *Metaphors We Live By*. Chicago: University of Chicago Press.

Loftus, E. 1988. *Memory: Surprising New Insights into How We Remember and Why We Forget*. Lanham, MD: Rowman and Littlefield.

McEvilley, T. 2002. *The Shape of Ancient Thought*. New York: Allworth Press.

McIntyre, A. 1985. *After Virtue*. London: Duckworth.

McRae, E. 2015. "Metabolizing Anger: A Tantric Buddhist Solution to the Problem of Moral Anger." *Philosophy East and West* 65:2, pp. 466–84.

McRae, E. 2018. "Anger and the Oppressed: Indo-Tibetan Buddhist Perspectives." In M. Cherry and O. Flanagan, eds., *The Moral Psychology of Anger*. Lanham, MD: Rowman and Littlefield, pp. 105–22.

Mendis, N.K.G. 1993. *The Questions of King Milinda: An Abridgment of the "Milindapañha."* Kandy: Buddhist Publication Society.

Metzinger, T. 2004. *Being No-One: The Self-Theory Model of Subjectivity*. Cambridge, MA: MIT Press/Bradford Books.

———. 2010. *The Ego Tunnel: The Science of the Mind and the Myth of the Self*. New York: Basic Books.

Moulton, C., and R. Epstein. 2005. "Self-Monitoring in Surgical Practice: Slowing Down When You Should." In H. Fry and R. Kneebone, eds., *Surgical Education, Advances in Medical Education*, vol. 2. Dordrecht: Springer, pp. 169–82.

Mukerji, A. C. 1938. *The Nature of Self*. Allahabad: The Indian Press.

Nagel, T. 1974. "What Is It Like to Be a Bat?" *The Philosophical Review* 83:4, pp. 435–50.

———. 1989. *The View from Nowhere*. New York: Oxford University Press.

Nhat Hanh, T. 1987. *Interbeing*. Berkeley: Parallax Press.

———. 1993. *Love in Action: Writings on Nonviolent Social Change*. Berkeley: Parallax Press.

———. 2005. *Being Peace*. Berkeley: Parallax Press.

———. 2017. *The Art of Living: Peace and Freedom in the Here and Now*. Berkeley: Parallax Press.

Nisbett, R., and L. Ross. 1980. *Human Inference.* Englewood Cliffs, NJ: Prentice-Hall.

Noice, H., and T. Noice. "Artistic Performance: Acting, Ballet, and Contemporary Dance." In Ericsson et al. (2006), pp. 489–504.

Olivelle, P. 2008. *The Upaniṣads.* New York: Oxford University Press.

Parfit, D. 1984. *Reasons and Persons.* Oxford: Oxford University Press.

Patrul Rinpoche. 2017. *Essential Jewel of Holy Practice.* Boston: Wisdom Publications.

Rawls, J. 1999. *A Theory of Justice.* Cambridge, MA: Harvard University Press.

Reddy, V. 2003. "On Being the Object of Attention: Implications for Self-Other Consciousness." *Trends in Cognitive Sciences* 7:9, pp. 397–402.

———. 2007. "Getting Back to the Rough Ground: Deception and 'Social Living.'" *Philosophical Transactions of the Royal Society B* 362, pp. 621–37.

Reddy, V. 2016. "Engagement: Looking beyond the Mirror to Understand Action Understanding," *British Journal of Developmental Psychology* 34, pp. 101–14.

———. 2018. "Why Engagement? A Second-Person Take on Social Cognition." In A. Newen, L. De Bruin, and S. Gallagher, eds., *The Oxford Handbook of 4E Cognition.* Oxford: Oxford University Press.

Ricoeur, P. 1995. *Oneself as Another.* Chicago: University of Chicago Press.

Rosenbaum. D., et al. 2006. "Perceptual-Motor Expertise." In Ericsson et al. (2006), pp. 505–22.

Schopenhauer, A. 2005. *Essay on the Freedom of the Will.* Chicago: Dover.

Schwitzgebel, E. 2011. *Perplexities of Consciousness.* Cambridge: MIT Press.

Sellars, W. 1954. "Some Reflections on Language Games." *Philosophy of Science* 21:3, pp. 204–28.

———. 1963. "Empiricism and the Philosophy of Mind." In W. Sellars, *Science Perception and Reality,* London: Routledge and Kegan Paul, pp. 129–94.

———. 1969. "Language as Thought and as Communication." *Philosophy and Phenomenological Research* 29:4, pp. 506–27.

Shantideva [Śāntideva]. 2006. *The Way of the Bodhisattva.* Padmakara Translation Group. Boston: Shambhala.

Sharf, R. 2005. "Ritual." In D. Lopez, ed., *Critical Terms for the Study of Buddhism.* Chicago: University of Chicago Press, pp. 245–69.

Siderits, M. 2017. *Personal Identity and Buddhist Philosophy: Empty Persons.* London: Routledge.

Siderits, M., E. Thompson, and D. Zahavi. 2011. *Self, No Self? Perspectives from Analytical, Phenomenological, and Indian Traditions.* Oxford: Oxford University Press.

Slingerland, E. 2007. *Effortless Action: Wu-wei as Conceptual Metaphor and Spiritual Ideal in Early China.* New York: Oxford University Press.

Sorabji, R. 2006. *Self: Ancient and Modern Insights about Individuality, Life, and Death.* Chicago: University of Chicago Press.

Stoler Miller, B. 1986. *The Bhagavad Gītā: Krishna's Counsel in Time of War.* New York: Bantam Books.

Strawson. G. 1997. "The Self." *Journal of Consciousness Studies* 4:5/6, pp. 405–28.

———. 2011a. "Radical Self-Awareness." In Siderits, Thompson, and Zavahi (2011), pp. 274–307.

———. 2011b. *Selves: An Essay on Revisionary Metaphysics.* Oxford: Oxford University Press.

Strawson, P. F. 2008. "Freedom and Resentment." In P. F. Strawson, *Freedom and Resentment and Other Essays.* London: Routledge, pp. 1–28.

Strohminger, N., and S. Nichols. 2014. "The Essential Moral Self." *Cognition* 131:1, pp. 159–71.

Thompson, E. 2010. *Mind in Life: Biology, Phenomenology, and the Sciences of Mind.* Cambridge, MA: Belknap Press.

———. 2011. "Self-No-Self: Memory and Reflexive Awareness." In Siderits, Thompson, and Zavahi (2011), pp. 157–75.

———. 2014. *Waking, Dreaming, Being: Self and Consciousness in Neuroscience, Meditation, and Philosophy.* New York: Columbia University Press.

———. 2020. *Why I Am Not a Buddhist.* New Haven: Yale University Press.

Thurman, R. 2014. *Tsong Khapa's Speech of Gold in "The Essence of True Eloquence."* Princeton: Princeton University Press.

Tolman, E. 1938. "Physiology, Psychology, and Sociology." *Psychological Review* 45:3, pp. 228–41.

Tsongkhapa. 2006. *Ocean of Reasoning: A Great Commentary on Nāgārjuna's "Mūlamadhyamakakārikā."* Trans. J. Garfield and N. Samten. New York: Oxford University Press.

Tzohar, R. 2018. *A Yogācāra Buddhist Theory of Metaphor.* New York: Oxford University Press.

Vygotsky, L. 1978. *Mind in Society: The Development of Higher Psychological Processes.* Cambridge, MA: Harvard University Press.

Wallace, A., and V. Wallace. 1997. *A Guide to the Bodhisattva Way of Life.* Boston: Wisdom Publications.

Watson, A. 2017. "Self or No-Self: The Ātman Debate in Classical Indian Philosophy." In J. Tuske, ed., *Indian Epistemology and Metaphysics.* London: Bloomsbury, pp. 293–318.

Watson, B. 1964. *Chuang Tzu: Basic Writings.* New York: Columbia University Press.

Westerhoff, J. 2020. *The Non-Existence of the Real World.* Oxford: Oxford University Press.

Williams, B. 1986. *Ethics and the Limits of Philosophy.* Cambridge, MA: Harvard University Press.

Williams, P. 2000. *The Reflexive Nature of Awareness: A Tibetan Madhyamaka Defence.* New Delhi: Motilal Banarsidass.

Wittgenstein, L. 1969. *On Certainty.* New York: Harper Torchbooks.

Wittgenstein, L. 2009. *Philosophical Investigations.* Boston: Wiley-Blackwell.

Yancy, G., and E. McRae, eds. 2019. *Buddhism and Whiteness.* Lanham, MD: Lexington Books.

Zahavi, D. 2008. *Subjectivity and Selfhood: Investigating the First-Person Perspective.* Cambridge, MA: MIT Press/Bradford Books.

Zahavi, D. 2011. "The Experiential Self: Objections and Clarifications." In Siderits, Thompson, and Zahavi (2011), pp. 56–78.

———. 2020. *Self-Awareness and Alterity: A Phenomenological Investigation.* Chicago: Northwestern University Press.

Zimmerman, A., and B. Kitsantis. 1987. "Developmental Phases in Self-Regulation: Shifting from Process Goals to Outcome Goals." *Journal of Educational Psychology,* 89:1, pp. 29–36.

INDEX

Actualizing the Fundamental Point, 112
Ahab, 159
ahaṃkāra, 87–88
agency, 37; nondual, 102–3, 107; and
   self, 21, 28, 49, 101–2, 125, 130, 171
agent causation, 5, 33, 102, 125–27
Aitken, R., 183n10
Anacker, A., 176n10
anger, 25, 125, 128–29, 184n9; Śāntideva
   on, 125, 128–29
anticipation, 63–66
Aristotle, 74–75
ātman, 2–5, 14, 29, 37, 52, 96, 149, 175n7,
   177nn1 and 2, 178n7, 185n4
Augustine of Hippo, 5, 126–27
awareness, 53, 71–72, 94–95, 102, 108,
   114, 141–43; Aristotle on, 74–75;
   Dharmakīrti on, 74–75; Dignāga
   on, 79; expert, 110; Kant on, 54;
   nondual, 103–4, 113; reflexivity of,
   67–81, 92, 95; Śāntideva on, 125–28;
   self and, 70–72, 78, 83, 89–96, 104,
   107; Strawson on, 68–70, 74; subjectivity and, 32–33, 114; and subject-
   object duality, 72–73, 75, 102, 114;
   Thompson on, 79–81, 89, 92–96,
   180n6, 181nn22 and 23, 182nn28 and 29

Baggins, B., 159
Baier, K., 183n2 (Chap. 7)

Baker, L. R., 185n3
Becker, E., 174n10
Beckwith, C., 173n1 (Preface)
Beilock, S., 183n7
Berkeley, G., 47
Bhagavad Gītā, 3, 173n4
Bhattacharyya, K. C., 179n9, 187n5
Bhushan, N., 179n9
binding problem, 55, 178n7
Bodhicāryāvatāra. See *How to Lead an*
   Awakened Life
Bolt, U., 8
Bommarito, N., 184n5
Boroditsky, L., 186n7
Bradley, F. H., 176n18
Brahmavihāras. See divine states
Buddhaghosa, 122
Buddhism, 17, 26, 28, 30, 35, 44, 73, 87,
   122–24, 133; and awareness, 180n11,
   183n3; Ganeri on, 174n7, 185n4;
   Garfield on, 173n2 (Preface), 176n10,
   184nn5 and 7; meditative practice
   in, 100; and no-self, 4, 13–17, 25, 79;
   and persons, 20, 149, 173n2 (Preface),
   175nn4 and 5, 177n5; and reflexivity,
   74, 79, 81, 179n4, 180nn11 and 14;
   and self, 3, 21, 42, 83, 174n7, 175nn6
   and 7, 176n12, 177n5, 178n7, 184n9,
   185n3; Thompson on, 96; and unity,
   179n13

Title! The Words (Ford poem, from Garfield, 2022)

The words for 'Woda'
'Alec's pilgrimage' are merely a
designation with no determinate reference
There is 'Alec'
There is 'Alec', who exists not as a self
but as a person
Who takes the reality of the world far greater
who has no essence, nothing behind 'his'
mind and body
The person denotes the complex,
constructed, socially embedded
psychosocial complex computers
'Alec is freed to experience 'himself' on
a 'self'. And as a 'self' not experience quit
There is no 'pilgrimage'. Take away 'Alec's
body', all 'pilgrimage' bodies and
there is nothing here
No pilgrimage destination
no 'goal'

A NOTE ON THE TYPE

This book has been composed in Arno, an Old-style serif typeface in the classic Venetian tradition, designed by Robert Slimbach at Adobe.